D0477344

English Country House

·E·C·C·E·N·T·R·I·C·S·

English Country House ·E·C·C·E·N·T·R·I·C·S·

David Long

with illustrations by Les Evans

Other books by David Long

Spectacular Vernacular: London's 100 Most Extraordinary Buildings

Tunnels, Towers & Temples: London's 100 Strangest Places

The Little Book of London

The Little Book of the London Underground

Blood Sweat and Tyres: The Little Book of the Automobile

When Did Big Ben First Bong?
101 questions answered about the greatest city on earth

Hidden City:
The Secret Alleys, Courts and Yards of London's Square Mile

London Underground: Architecture, Design and History

First published 2012

The History Press
The Mill, Brimscombe Port
Stroud, Gloucestershire, GL5 2QG
www.thehistorypress.co.uk

British Library Cataloguing in Publication Data.
A catalogue record for this book is available from the British Library.

ISBN 978 0 7524 6731 3

Typesetting and origination by The History Press
Printed in Great Britain

·C·O·N·T·E·N·T·S·

Introduction   9

Bedfordshire
Woburn Abbey   11
Berkshire
Ashdown House   13
Basildon Park   14
Cliveden   17
Buckinghamshire
Dinton Hall   19
Hartwell House   20
Stowe   21
Waddesdon Manor   23
West Wycombe Park   24
Cambridgeshire
Kimbolton Castle   27
Wimpole Hall   29
Cumbria
Lowther Castle   32
Derbyshire
Calke Abbey   34
Chatsworth House   36
Elvaston Castle   39
Renishaw Hall   41
Devon
Castle Drogo   43
Knightshayes Court   45
Dorset
Clouds Hill   48
St Giles House   50
Essex
Belhus   53
Champion Lodge   55
Hedingham Castle   57

Gloucestershire
Snowshill Manor 60
Hertfordshire
Ashridge 63
Hatfield House 65
Letchworth Hall 66
Lockleys 68
North Mymms Park 70
Tring Park 72
Kent
Chartwell 75
Chevening House 77
Cold Harbour 78
Down House 81
Howletts 84
Knole House 87
Mount Morris 88
Sissinghurst 90
Lancashire
Birchin Bower 93
Lincolnshire
Gunby Hall 95
Harlaxton Manor 97
Middlesex
Bentley Priory 99
Trent Park 100
Norfolk
Abbots Hall 103
Northamptonshire
Deene Park 105
Easton Neston 107
Rushton Lodge 109
Northumberland
Cragside 112
Nottinghamshire
Bestwood Lodge 115
Bunny Hall 116
Clumber Park 118
Welbeck Abbey 120

Oxfordshire

Faringdon House 122

Friar Park 123

Swinbrook House 125

Thame Park 126

Rutland

Exton Park 128

Shropshire

Attingham Park 129

Halston Hall 130

Mawley Hall 131

Suffolk

Ickworth House 133

Stoke College 134

Surrey

Clandon Park 136

Devil's Punch Bowl 137

Painshill Park 139

Witley Park 140

Sussex

Batemans 142

Brightling Park 143

Petworth House 144

Warwickshire

Coton House 146

West Midlands

Tettenhall Towers 148

Wiltshire

Fonthill Abbey 150

Worcestershire

Broadway Tower 152

Yorkshire

Sledmere House 155

Walton Hall 156

Note: The majority of the houses described are opened to the public at specified times of year, those owned by the National Trust being marked in the text (NT) and others in the care of English Heritage (EH).

By 1965 the old county of Middlesex – England's smallest but for Rutland – was largely subsumed into Central London with small portions allotted to Hertfordshire and Surrey.

⬧I⬧N⬧T⬧R⬧O⬧D⬧U⬧C⬧T⬧I⬧O⬧N⬧

L ord Monboddo, a judge, believed men were born with tails but that this was concealed by a conspiracy of midwives who cut them off at birth. Sir Francis Galton, using a system no-one but he could understand, spent years compiling a map of the country showing the distribution of its most beautiful inhabitants and the really ugly ones. And as recently as 1976 a retired schoolmaster called Ernest Digweed left £26,000 for the Second Coming which 'the Public Trustee . . . upon obtaining proof which shall satisfy them of His identity, shall pay to Lord Jesus Christ'.

Ostentatious or absurdly secretive, crazily ambitious, insanely inventive, pathologically reclusive or just faintly ridiculous, there is something irresistible about eccentrics and rarely more so than when it comes to the builders and burrowers, the collectors, hoarders, faddists and strange obsessives who have created, occupied and occasionally lost many of the great country houses which form such an important part of Britain's cultural inheritance.

Eccentricity is by no means a preserve of the rich, aristocratic and landed, but for those determined to turn their backs on the mainstream, a large fortune and an isolated country estate certainly makes it easier. Insulated by walls of stone and the wealth of oligarchs, such men (and occasionally women) preside over personal fiefdoms and are answerable to no-one. It's an environment which provides ample scope for eccentricities and idiosyncrasies to thrive, and as can be seen in the following pages many grasped the opportunity with both hands as they set off on their own, peculiar personal odysseys

Among their number one finds visionaries and mad men, builders and destroyers, and collectors who ruined themselves in the process. It was a Spaniard, the Romantic painter Francisco Goya, who insisted 'fantasy abandoned by reason produces impossible monsters' – but more than 400 years of English eccentricity has also thrown up things of wonder, value and beauty which we can still enjoy today.

David Long, Suffolk, 2012
www.davidlong.info

Bedfordshire

Woburn's saviour was very much the 13th Duke of Bedford (1917–2002) who, after being disinherited for marrying beneath him, took the courageous step of renting the place from his own trustees in the hope he could earn enough to settle the estate's enormous death duties.

His grandfather Herbrand, the 11th Duke, was a famously mean-minded and miserable misanthrope who in the words of his eventual successor 'lived a cold, aloof existence, isolated from the outside world by a mass of servants, sycophants and an eleven-mile wall.' With major landholdings in central London, and two houses in Belgrave Square which he rarely visited, he famously sold off Covent Garden and put the money into Russian shares which were immediately wiped out by the Bolshevik Revolution.

Herbrand rarely spoke, but that was alright as his duchess was stone deaf. After waiting until she was a pensioner before deciding to learn to fly, she took off at the age of 71 and was never seen again (she's assumed to have taken a wrong turning instead of flying back home where a servant had helpfully stencilled the word 'Woburn' on the roof to guide her in).

Hastings, their only child, was born in a derelict crofter's cottage while his parents were out shooting, and inherited his fair share of peculiarities from both sides of the family. To these he added a penchant for extreme right-wing politics – the House of Lords eventually passed a motion that 'the Duke of Bedford no longer be heard' – and such a preference for parrots over people that his own son described him as the loneliest person he had ever met. For company he also kept a pet spider which he hand-fed roast beef, and 'incapable of giving or receiving love, utterly self-centred and opinionated,' when he died it was of a gunshot wound, self-inflicted and almost certainly intentional.

Prior to this, and in order to supplement their own meagre rations, his children were forced to steal food from parrots – mostly chocolates, which the birds adored – and were denied the opportunity to go to school because their father had been bullied at Eton. After marrying a divorcee the future 13th Duke was then cut off without a penny, finding work as rent collector in London's East End and a reporter on the downmarket *Daily Express*.

By the time he inherited, aged 36 in 1953, the abbey had been empty for thirteen years and was shockingly run-down. Priceless artworks were stacked around the walls like a warehouse, and those parts which had not already been demolished were riddled with rot.

The duke realised the only way to finance its repair would be to open Woburn to the public, and believing his ancestral possessions were 'just plain boring' he looked for new ways to give visitors their money's worth including a children's playground, a shooting gallery, an antiques market and a bingo hall.

Fellow dukes looked on in horror, but Bedford revealed himself to be a real showman as well as an entrepreneur. Special weekends were laid on for nudists, thereby guaranteeing yards of newspaper coverage, and recognising that people preferred seeing a living duke to a dead one by Van Dyke, 50 guineas would buy a bed for the night together with what His Grace described as 'tea in golden teapots and that sort of thing'.

Never one to pass up on free publicity, he twice acted the part of a duke on screen, sold the television rights to his third marriage, appeared in a commercial for shoe polish and even admitted that when he was prosecuted for careless driving, the fact that the police had identified him by his numberplate (DOB 1) will have done nothing to harm Woburn's takings.

Eventually he handed the place over to his son and retired to Monte Carlo, hardly the usual destination for a duke but then as he himself always said, he was never 'an old-fashioned grouse-shooting sort'.

Berkshire

Owned by the National Trust but at the time of writing leased to a rock guitarist, the tall and narrow Ashdown House is a romantic place with a romantic history. It was built in the 1660s by William, 1st Lord Craven, for the unrequited love of his life, Elizabeth of Bohemia.

Elizabeth was the sister of Charles I, nicknamed the 'Winter Queen' not for her frosty temperament but because she was forced into exile with her husband Frederick V. This followed his defeat by the Habsburg Emperor at the Battle of White Mountain, in November 1620.

In the long run the family were to have their day: a favourite son was to drown but their daughter Sophia was to become the founder of the Hanoverian dynasty, which held sway in Britain from George I in 1714 until the death of Victoria nearly two centuries later. In 1620 their plight was desperate, however, and after barely more than a year on the throne Frederick and Elizabeth found themselves stripped of their ancestral lands and effectively stateless.

Fighting a rearguard action, Frederick eventually established a government-in-exile, basing himself in The Hague although thereafter he seems to have spent more time hunting and taking country walks than actually overseeing the administration. Within ten years he was anyway dead of pestilential fever, and his widow eventually returned home to England where she had the good fortune to find herself under the protection of the devoted and wealthy Lord Craven.

A soldierly type who had fallen in love with her while fighting for her husband, one likes to think his motivations were entirely honourable for although Pepys admitted to being shocked by his bawdy language in other regards the old soldier seems to have been driven by wholly chivalrous impulses. According to legend he decided to build Ashdown House after hearing that the deposed queen was 'longing to live in quiet', presumably choosing a style not unlike a typically tall, narrow Dutch townhouse in the belief that this would enable Her Majesty to live in surroundings at once comfortable and quietly familiar.

He furnished it beautifully too, including one painting by Sir Peter Lely (sadly now sold) entitled *An Allegory of Love* that is said to represent the lovelorn Lord Craven and the object of his adoration. It is also believed that he chose this spot high on the rolling, windswept Berkshire Downs as a safe refuge from plague-hit London.

Sadly, true or not, it was a gambit which in the end failed to matter. While Lord Craven enjoyed the satisfaction of knowing that he was providing for his love's every wish, while staying at his London home in Drury Lane, Elizabeth of Bohemia contracted an infection and died before Ashdown House was ready to receive her. Craven was heartbroken, and though he lived to be ninety years old he never married, preferring to live in seclusion surrounded by Elizabeth's paintings and papers and other personal effects.

Successive generations of Cravens were to remain at Ashdown until the mid-1950s when it was handed to the National Trust by the 7th Countess. Since then much work has been carried out to make good the fabric which took a bruising during a period of military occupation in the war, and then again following a fire which gutted it in 1984. Now restored and tenanted, limited public access to the house and grounds is possible at certain times of the year.

BASILDON PARK, Lower Basildon, nr Reading (NT)

Over the years any number of British buildings have gone missing. In 1930 Henry Ford found a 350-year-old house he liked in the Cotswolds and had it shipped back home to Michigan. In the 1960s London Bridge followed it across the Atlantic to be rebuilt in Lake Havasu City, Arizona. And in 2007 London's old Baltic Exchange – a Grade II listed beauty blown up by the IRA and then swept away to make room for the Gherkin – was snapped up by someone wishing to reassemble it in Estonia.

It seems incredible now, but once upon a time eighteenth-century Basildon Park looked like it might go the same way. In 1771 the estate had been purchased by Sir Francis Sykes Bt, who having made a fortune as an Indian 'nabob', planned to spend most of it building a new house for himself. Unfortunately almost the day work on it began he lost the equivalent of £14 million when shares in the East India Company crashed. Then two years later was forced to hand back another chunk of cash following allegations of corruption during his time in India.

By the time he died in 1804 most of the money was long gone and, while the house was completed, the principal rooms were bare and unfurnished. The 2nd Baronet then survived his father by a matter of weeks, leaving a heavily mortgaged Basildon to a five-year-old, who by the age of fourteen was himself spending enormous sums of borrowed money entertaining his new best friend, the notoriously profligate Prince Regent.

In 1829 the estate was back on the market, but failed to sell because this latest Sir Francis refused to consider anything less than £100,000 (approximately £80 million today). Between times his family solved their immediate money worries by renting the house out and moving somewhere cheaper, and it was during this period that Lady Sykes had an ill-judged affair with a friend of Charles Dickens. Not unreasonably Sir Francis objected, but in so doing caused such a scandal that the author took revenge by appropriating his name for the odious 'Bill Sikes' in *Oliver Twist*.

By 1830 Sir Francis had been persuaded to accept £93,000 from James Morrison, a successful Hampshire merchant whose collections included not only English paintings and continental old masters but

Charles Dickens

Bill Sykes

other estates in Kent, Wiltshire, Yorkshire and Scotland. He could certainly afford another one and Basildon Park – at least until 1916, when it was turned over to the Army – now entered something of a golden period.

By 1920 Morrison's grandson was head of the family. Injured at the Somme and awarded the DSO, he spent a time improving the estate but rarely stayed except for lavish shooting parties. Eventually his money ran out too – married three times, he liked to live well – and in 1928 he sold up to a neighbour. Unfortunately the neighbour wanted the land more than the house, and after stripping out a few choice fireplaces and door surrounds, Basildon Park was passed on to one George Ferdinando.

Ferdinando immediately advertised Basildon Park for sale at $1,000,000, the price to include the cost of dismantling it and shipping the parts across Atlantic where it could be reassembled for 'any patriotic American wishing to benefit his native state by presenting this imposing building . . . ready for occupation as a private residence, museum, college building or public library.'

The Great Depression meant buyers were hard to come by, and once a caretaker helped himself to lead from the roof the house began badly to deteriorate. Returning home Ferdinando briefly lived in one corner of what was now a leaky ruin, and perhaps in the belief that he was rescuing them, sold many of the more vulnerable fixtures and fittings to New York's Waldorf-Astoria Hotel and Metropolitan Museum of Art, and the Museum of Fine Arts, Boston.

Thereafter Basildon's second salvation had to wait until another period of military occupation (1939–45) after which it was sold for the final time. By chance the buyers were the son and daughter-in-law of the neighbour who had acquired the land in 1928, the 2nd Lord Iliffe and his wife lovingly returning Basildon Park to its former glory and then presenting it to the National Trust.

CLIVEDEN, nr Taplow (NT)

Cliveden was created for one duke, let to another, rebuilt by a third, and bought by a fourth, yet to most these days the best-known association is with the Astors and the names of its illustrious ducal quartet – Buckingham, Gloucester, Sutherland and Westminster – are all but buried in its past.

When he took on the estate from his widowed mother-in-law, the 1st Duke of Westminster already had a seat at Eaton Hall in Cheshire but wanted money to support his growing charitable commitments. William Waldorf Astor had money ($175 million from his father) but needed a seat and in 1873 found what he wanted in Cliveden, for which he paid $1.2 million.

For an American as hell-bent as Astor on acquiring the trappings and titles of an English aristocrat, Cliveden was a catch. Designed by Sir Charles Barry (architect of the Houses of Parliament) it was built on the spot where 'Rule Britannia' was first performed, high above what for many is the very loveliest stretch of the River Thames.

The price included most of the contents too, although not the valuable paintings – which were returned when His Grace realised these had been left behind – and not the 200-year-old visitors book, which Astor nevertheless refused to hand back despite repeated requests to do so.

He then spent an incredible £6,000,000 fixing the place up, acquiring antique wainscoting from Madame de Pompadour's Château d'Asnières, a fountain and a balustrade from the Villa Borghese, and various old Roman sarcophagi and statuary which were placed aroun the grounds. Astor also built tall walls around the park to stop members of the public boating on his lake, hence the joke locally that his name was really 'Walled-Orf'".

It was his son, another Waldorf, who really put Cliveden on the map though – he and his teetotal bride Nancy, the first woman to sit in the Commons, gathering together a group of influential individuals known as the 'Cliveden Set'. Accused of being pro-Nazi, most were really just supporters of Neville Chamberlain's appeasement movement although the arrival of the odious Sir Oswald and Lady Mosley – who brought a petrol can full of dry martini to jolly up the weekend – did little to quell the rumours.

Cliveden's second brush with scandal – and one can only imagine what Christian Scientist Nancy might have made of it – hit the headlines in 1963. With all the right ingredients – call girls, glamour, aristocracy and espionage –when the Minister for War, John Profumo, admitted lying to Parliament, Macmillan's government was doomed. Having an affair was bad for a married cabinet minister; worse still Profumo shared his mistress with Captain Yevgeny Ivanov, assistant Russian military attaché and almost certainly a spy.

By this time Cliveden had been gifted to the nation and, when the 3rd Viscount Astor died five years later, the National Trust moved in, restoring its peerless setting and giving the house a new lease of life as a fine hotel. The swimming pool where Profumo met Christine Keeler met is still in use, but there is as yet no sign of the duke's visitors book.

DINTON HALL, Dinton

A large, gabled sixteenth-century brick house built by William Warham (1450–1532) – variously Master of the Rolls, Lord Chancellor and Archbishop of Canterbury – in 1617 Dinton Hall came into the possession of the roundhead, lawyer and regicide Simon Mayne, although today its strongest association is with John Bigg, the so-called Dinton Hermit.

Bigg served as a clerk to Mayne, and saw him through an exceptionally difficult period following the Restoration. Along with the other prominent Parliamentarians who had signed the King's death warrant, Mayne was hunted down by an understandably aggrieved Charles II who was keen to avenge his father's execution.

Mayne foolishly tried to hide away at Dinton, surely the first place anyone would look, and on being discovered was dragged back to London, and locked in the Tower where he fell ill – too ill to walk to the scaffold – and died. Bigg took the news badly, moving out of the hall and into a nearby cave where he settled down to spend the rest of his life.

Today such behaviour would have earned a diagnosis of clinical depression, but in seventeenth-century Buckinghamshire it saw Bigg recast as a local celebrity. Though not without means, Bigg chose to live very simply, refusing to beg for alms but happy to accept the charity of villagers and visitors who fed and watered him for the next thirty-five years.

Once handsome, he very soon lost his youthful appearance, something not helped by his choice of apparel which included a peculiar, twin-peaked hooded cape and a succession of leather bottles which he hung from his waist to store the milk, strong ale and small beer which he received from local benefactors.

As time went by this singular appearance was exaggerated by his habit of making and mending his own clothes. Living in a cave, wear and tear was considerable, and as Bigg continued to sew patch onto patch onto patch, his garments – often as many as twelve layers thick – came to resemble little more than a heaps of scraps thrown together.

Visitors to his cave were encouraged to bring any suitable scraps with them when they called, Biggs performing a similar trick with his

shoes which were soon well over six inches wide with new pieces of leather being nailed on each time an older piece wore through. Sadly, if unsurprisingly, none of the clothes has survived, but since 2003 a pair of shoes has been available for inspection at the Ashmolean Museum at Oxford, each one thought to comprise as many as 1,000 pieces of leather.

HARTWELL HOUSE, Hartwell, nr Aylesbury (NT)

Another National Trust property run as an hotel, the Hartwell estate is mentioned in Domesday – it was owned by the bastard son of William the Bastard – although the present house is largely of the seventeenth century.

A number of historical figures are connected to the Hampden and Lee families which owned it from about 1650 until the 1930s, including the American Civil War general, Robert E. Lee, and the founder of the Royal Meteorological Society which held its inaugural meeting in the library in 1850. The most interesting resident was merely a tenant, however – the exiled King Louis XVIII of France who leased it from 1809–14.

As befits a Bourbon, Louis attempted to live in the style to which any king would have been accustomed, arriving with around 100 attendants, courtiers and protégés and paying £500 per annum rent.

Unfortunately Louis was broke, so broke the British taxpayer was already bailing him out, and in truth Hartwell was way too small. Partitions had hastily to be erected to divide state apartments into smaller, more private ones, and all over the estate various outbuildings and animal shelters were turned over to individuals who before the revolution occupied some of the most splendid palaces in France. (The royal chickens were at the same time kept on the roof, although this was probably because His Majesty wished to keep an eye on the eggs and not because their coops had been lent to distressed nobles.)

Hartwell's owner, Sir George Lee Bt, seemed not to mind what was going on, instead remaining philosophical and admitting he was on the whole 'satisfied with the remuneration of the British government.' Despite the death of his queen in 1810 Louis seems to have managed to keep his spirits up too, although his brother was reportedly prone to deep depressions. It may have helped that Louis was able to walk in the grounds with his friend Gustav IV, formerly of Sweden, the two of them able to share the lonely experience of being deposed, exiled and indigent, a writer in *Bell's Weekly Messenger* noting 'the rare and not unaffecting sight of two ex-kings promenading the groves together, and ministering, apparently, to each other, condolence and consolation.'

English visitors were rare, and on the whole the French kept themselves to themselves, licking their wounds and waiting for news that Napoleon had come a cropper so they could return home. Occasionally, to the delight of the people of Berkhamsted, Louis would stop in the town en route to London and was said to have struck up a friendship with the landlord's daughter at the King's Arms. She later visited him in Paris, but afterwards wrote to a newspaper insisting that the King's Arms at Berkhamsted were the only king's arms into which she had fallen.

STOWE, nr Buckingham (NT)

Home to conceivably the best situated school in the country if not the best *per se*, the house at Stowe may be only rarely opened to the public but for much of the year the grounds are accessible – and for many they are the best thing about the place.

With more follies than any other landscape garden – nearly thirty-five of them at the last count, a good proportion of which are temples

– Stowe was the creation of the 1st Viscount Cobham, the aptly named Sir Richard Temple (1669–1749), a leading Whig politician who distinguished himself during the Duke of Marlborough's campaigns in the War of the Spanish Succession.

As a pun on the name, his motto was Templa Quam Dilecta – 'HOW BEAUTIFUL ARE THY TEMPLES' – something he and his descendants took to heart at Stowe where they employed many of the leading architects and landscape designers of the period.

The latter included Charles Bridgeman, the inventor of the ha-ha; Capability Brown, obviously; Humphrey Repton; William Kent and J.C. Loudon. When it came to architects the obvious choice was a fellow soldier, Sir John Vanbrugh, and when he died Giacomo Leoni and James Gibbs were brought in to continue beautifying the estate.

Visitors came from far and wide to see the results, including the aforementioned exiles, Louis XVIII and Gustav IV; also the Prince of Wales, Christian VII of Denmark, and two future Tsars – Alexander and Nicholas I. One wonders, however, how many of them understood the political subtext to the gardens, or indeed realised that their creator was interested in far more than simply providing somewhere beautiful for him and his guests to enjoy.

The Temple of Modern Virtue, for example, was deliberately left a ruin as a comment on what Lord Cobham saw as the ruinous policies associated with the ministry of the despised Sir Robert Walpole. Unfortunately it has since disappeared, but the complementary Temple of Ancient Virtues still stands and was designed around the same time to celebrate the many admirable qualities that Cobham thought were under threat. A third temple by William Kent, an elegant stone curve dedicated to 'British Worthies', contains the busts of those whom Cobham felt conformed to his own world view, including the writer Alexander Pope who was also strongly opposed to Prime Minister Walpole.

If all this makes Cobham sound a tad obsessive, not to say slightly vindictive, then consider this story of what happened to a couple of young poachers caught on the estate in 1748. Among landowners Cobham was known to come down hard on this kind of thing, so when the wives of the men heard that they had been caught going after his deer, both of them presented themselves at the big house and respectfully asked for an audience.

A little surprisingly they were received with some warmth, before being ushered into the nobleman's presence. After making their appeal, both were assured by Lord Cobham – now an old man of eighty – that of course the men would be returned to their wives and children, and that he would see to it personally that they were not kept waiting long.

He kept his promise too, but neglected to mention that the two men would be returned in burial shrouds as they had already been hauled off to the courthouse in Buckingham. Following a brief hearing both had been 'drawn through the town streets to a neighbouring common, and there done to death amid the yelling of an execution mob that had gathered to feast its eyes on the sight of their agony'.

Locally there are still those who maintain that the vicious viscount went on to commemorate the encounter by erecting statues of the two dead men in his park, each one supporting a dead deer. This could well be true – as a politician he had strongly supported the introduction of the notorious Black Acts which dramatically increased the number of capital offences – but happily (if they existed) these grisly memorials have long since disappeared.

WADDESDON MANOR, Waddesdon, nr Aylesbury (NT)

A fairytale neo-Renaissance-style château, Waddesdon was conceived in 1874 by the lonely and prematurely widowed Baron Ferdinand de Rothschild, a member of the famous banking dynasty who was looking for somewhere to house his extensive collections of old master drawings, important French royal furniture, Sèvres porcelain, Beauvais tapestries, Savonnerie carpets and – more curiously – theatrical costumes.

In France Baron James de Rothschild had chosen an English architect so here in England it was perhaps only to be expected that Baron Ferdinand should plump for a Frenchman. He chose the exotically named Gabriel-Hippolyte Alexandre Destailleur, and for its setting a once-bare hillside rising to around 600ft above sea level.

Le Baron was out hunting when he first laid eyes on the unpromising, misshapen cone of Lodge Hill, a place where, in his own words, 'there was not a bush to be seen, nor was there a bird to be heard.' Making the owner an offer he could not refuse, he set about levelling the summit (in the manner of a giant soft-boiled egg) before planting the resulting plateau with trees and rare shrubs which he acquired in immense numbers.

Some of these came from other estates, such as Woburn Abbey and Claydon; others Rothschild collected himself from as far afield as Algiers. The total may not have been quite the 1,000,000 trees of legend, but nearly a century and a half later the effect is undeniably magnificent and a lasting tribute to its creator's botanical interests and knowledge of horticulture.

For the house Destailleur chose to copy stylistic elements from the royal Château de Chambord, although with the leitmotif very definitely the last word in luxury – the windows in the staircase towers were glazed unlike the sixteenth-century originals. Rothschild similarly asked for all the eighteenth-century chandeliers to be converted to run on electric power, such a novelty at the time that Queen Victoria is said to have spent more than ten minutes flicking a switch from on to off and back again.

The cost, needless to say, was enormous and included the construction of 14 miles of track and a private stream railway to lug hundreds of tons of Bath stone to the hill. Hundreds laboured for months on end, with teams of sixteen Percheron horses brought specially from France to manoeuvre giant oaks, beeches and conifers into position. Involving the removal of literally millions of tons of mud and spoil, with fresh water piped miles from the Chilterns, in all the project took some seven years.

Rothschild had just nine years to enjoy it before he died, but it is doubtful whether he ever did. The act of creation may have been something to relish, and among his shrubs, trees and orchids he was content, but when it came to entertaining he was an uneasy host. The future 27th Earl of Crawford noted how his 'hands always itch with nervousness' and how 'his clock for which he gave £25,000, his escritoire for which £30,000 was paid, his statuary, his china, his super collections . . . gimcracks, he calls them – all these things give him meagre satisfaction.'

WEST WYCOMBE PARK, West Wycombe (NT)

The founding father of what became known as the Hell Fire Club, Sir Francis Dashwood (1708–81) and friends used to gather at West Wycombe Park. This secretive sodality comprised a number of apparently wildly dissipated aristocrats who were said to celebrate
, delight in performing acts of 'gross lewdness and daring
desecrated altars, and to eat strange food served by naked
they later pressed their most disgusting desires.

however, is that most of the stories which have come
the years now sound so corny that one wonders whether

Dashwood's fabled wickedness was simply a contrivance got up to compensate for his boring daytime job as Postmaster-General. (He was Chancellor the Exchequer too, but only briefly once a rumour started circulating that he could not manage 'a bar bill of five figures'.)

Privately Sir Francis was at least a bit of a prankster: he and a chum once released a monkey in church which the congregation took to be Satan, and at West Wycombe he kept a replica Spanish galleon on the lake (complete with captain) for the amusement of his guests. But today he is chiefly remembered as the instigator of a series of fascinating follies which he built around the park and estate at West Wycombe.

Of these the strangest is perhaps the golden ball which sits on top of the fourteenth-century church, a feature added in the early 1760s and accessible only by ladder. Large enough to seat six for dinner, Hell Fire enthusiasts maintain the club met here to perform their sinister rituals and that the trees in the surrounding park were planted in such a way as to form patterns of vulgarity when viewed from above....

Elsewhere Sir Francis also built a mausoleum assisted by the wonderfully named John Bastard and using funds provided by Lord Melcombe to commemorate George III's emergence from madness. There is also another, wonderful flint-knapped church, which on close˘ inspection turns out to be an elegantly decorated cottage built to b˘ estate workers.

Since Dashwood's death in 1781 there has been nothi˘ match him, although the family has continued to thre˘ from time to time. The 3rd Baronet, for example, seen˘

Wycombe so much that he sold off half the furniture, while the 4th went bankrupt after hosting a teetotal festival in the grounds and giving the proceeds away to temperance campaigners.

By contrast the 7th Baronet turned out to be a drunken sheep farmer living in New Zealand, and when the 10th inherited he too started selling bits off including an important state bed (which realised just £58) and the neighbouring village. Fortunately his wife liked West Wycombe more than he did (indeed rather more than she did him) and in a bid to protect the house from further depredations chose to live separately at the other end from her husband rather than seek a divorce.

Undeterred he tried selling up, and when that failed West Wycombe was given to the National Trust to the great displeasure of the son and heir. Inheriting what remained twenty-three years later, the 11th Baronet gamely attempted to build a new village to replace the one his father had disposed of, but in the end had to content himself with buying back as much of the old furniture as he could find in order to restock a house which his family still occupies but no longer owns.

Cambridgeshire

KIMBOLTON CASTLE, Kimbolton

Since the first was created in 1337 approximately 500 individuals have been granted the right to call themselves duke, although barely two dozen of the exalted survive today. The dukedom of Manchester has so far escaped joining the ranks of these distinctive extinctions, but remains one of the lesser known. In part this may be because they have sold their seat – Kimbolton Castle is now a school – and because the present and 13th Duke prefers to live quietly and unobtrusively in California.

Briefly the Manchesters were better known, but largely thanks to the efforts of the 12th, a man once memorably described as the single best 'one-man argument against the hereditary rights of peers' and who by any reckoning was clearly something of a bounder.

Angus Charles Drogo Montagu (1938–2002) was married three times, although this is in itself hardly exceptional as it was long ago noted that divorce is far more common among the titled than the untitled, and that the higher the rank the more ex-wives there tend to be scattered around the place. That said, Angus was slightly unusual in that he married a £15 a week typist where most dukes at the very least tend to seek out wealthy heiresses.

His real distinction, however, was acquisition of an altogether different title – 'Prisoner 19127-018' – which is how he was known while serving time for financial fraud at the Federal Correctional Institution, Petersburg, Virginia.

At the time it was argued that his crime was to be too stupid to realise what he was up to, or to appreciate that he was being used by minds marginally brighter (and perhaps more crooked) than his own. Indeed at one of several trials an Old Bailey judge even went so far as to note that 'on a business scale of one to ten, the Duke is one or less, and even that flatters him'.

Too poor not to work, and with too great a sense of entitlement to do anything worthwhile, Angus had early on decided to trade on his title wherever he could – and before long he found himself in trouble.

Initially he was not so much eccentric as deeply naff. Like a lottery winner unable to come to terms with sudden wealth, what little common sense he may once have had seemed to desert him completely on inheriting. Inventing a courageous military career for himself at

Suez (when actually he had still been at school), his boasts included an entirely imaginary friendship with the Queen and a trip to China in the 1960s when he was shown the famous Terracotta Army by Chairman Mao himself – even though the figures were not unearthed until 1974.

Knowing little and caring even less for the Montagus' illustrious history – the name Drogo commemorates a presumed link with Drogo de Monte Acuto who arrived with the Conqueror – the new duke was nevertheless a great one for bringing up a version of it whenever possible. Frequent conversations with friends would habitually start with the words 'When I became a duke,' as if this had somehow transformed him into a completely different person. In fact his circumstances were very little altered, with family trustees allowing him only a very modest flat in Bedford and a small allowance which he quickly frittered away by hiring limos where a bus might have been more appropriate.

His notion of what a duke should look like was also curious, the somewhat tubby peer's preference being for shoes fastened with Velcro rather than laces and nasty line in 'drip-dry' blazers. These he attempted to smarten up with regimental ties and service buttons to which he was not entitled, but few were fooled and even his own solicitor noted that 'Angus was always treated with suspicion, even before going to prison.'

His only regular income seems to have been the attendance allowance due from the House of Lords when he was in London, although when tempted by a variety of dodgy friends to step outside his (admittedly very limited) comfort zone, Angus quickly came to believe he was a good businessman who was bound to make a fortune. It didn't take long for him to put his name to a scheme he was ill-equipped either to understand or to execute, and to the delight of the popular press the duke soon found himself back in court. This time it was in Florida, where he was charged with attempting to defraud the Tampa Bay Lightning ice hockey team of nearly $2 million.

To a man who liked to stand on ceremony it must have been a source of some anguish to be referred to throughout the trial as 'Mr Montagu', but perhaps preferable to the final summing-up by his own defence team who described his character as more dupe than duke. In the end he was found guilty on five counts of fraud, drawing a sentence of thirty-three months and serving just over two years while working in the prison laundry.

After his release he returned to his little flat in Bedford, finding work as an occasional, unofficial tour guide taking (largely American) groups around well-known tourist attractions such as Stratford-upon-Avon and Warwick Castle. He made the best of it, and always insisted

his clients were 'honoured to see an English Duke or Lord, and once you put them at ease they're wonderful people.' It all sounded a bit tacky, even for an ex-jailbird, but there was one even greater indignity still to be visited on poor old Angus.

Always stout and now decidedly corpulent, on 25 July 2002 Angus suffered what was to prove a fatal heart attack. He called an ambulance, and one duly arrived, but in order to get the 20 stone patient out of the flat it was necessary to summon a crane. The last public appearance of His Grace Angus Charles Drogo Montagu, 12th Duke of Manchester, involved the somewhat unedifying spectacle of a sixty-three-year-old being winched through a window. Needless to say the papers loved it.

WIMPOLE HALL, Wimpole (NT)

Owned at various different times by a knight, a baronet, a couple of viscounts, a countess in the making, seven earls and a duke, the magnificent Wimpole Hall estate nevertheless owes its survival into the present century to a commoner: Elsie Bambridge. The wife of Captain George Bambridge, and Rudyard Kipling's daughter, she leased and then bought what by 1938 had been allowed to deteriorate into little more than a bleak and empty shell, spending the best part of four decades piecing it back together before passing it on to the National Trust.

From 1740 to 1895 Wimpole had been the seat of the Earls of Hardwicke, for a while a quite exceptional dynasty which descended from a successful Kentish lawyer and over a period of several decades produced an admiral in the service of both the King and Nicholas I of Russia, a Home Secretary, two Fellows of the Royal Society, numerous Privy Councillors, not one but two Lord Chancellors, and a Lord Lieutenant of Ireland. For more than a century things seemed to be nicely on the up for the family, but then in 1873 the 5th Earl inherited Wimpole Hall and all that went with it – and very quickly turned out to be at best a rich twit and at worst a thoroughly bad egg.

Before coming into the earldom Charles Phillip Yorke (1836–97) was known by courtesy as Viscount Royston but by his friends and gossipmongers as 'Champagne Charlie'. Of this he was indeed the original, and the inspiration for Victorian music hall song of the same name, a comment on his extravagant lifestyle which he gleefully pursued at any and every cost to him and his family.

That said, the 5th Earl was not at first a complete waste of space. Admittedly this was an age when the aristocracy still had its hands on most of the levers of power, but before being elevated to the House of Lords the young Yorke was for ten years the Member for Cambridgeshire. At the same time he was an effective Comptroller to the Royal Household under Disraeli, and held the post of Master of the Buckhounds which meant his presence was required at Ascot where he was Her Majesty's official representative.

Unfortunately Lord Hardwicke was also something of a gambler, meaning his presence at the track came at quite a cost; so too did spending time in London where he had plenty more opportunities to gamble away the family fortune as an habitué of White's, among the most reckless of the St James's Street clubs when it came to high-stakes gambling.

Wagers here would be made on literally anything – the likelihood of George III recovering from insanity, for example, or an aspect of society tittle-tattle such as whether one duchess might outlive another. The wins could be huge too – the Duke of Portland won a phenomenal £200,000 at one sitting, keeping a clear head by drinking only water – but so could the losses. George Harley Drummond played there only once but was forced to resign from the family bank after losing £20,000 in an evening, and Sir John Bland of Kippax Park in Yorkshire actually killed himself after realising his gambling debts exceeded the value of his vast landholdings.

The scale of Hardwicke's losses at the club were not as high as Bland's, but then neither was he that rich. By 1894 he was in dire straits and keen to sell. Unfortunately no-one was keen to buy Wimpole at any price, let alone the £300,000 Hardwicke needed. Eventually the 2nd Lord Robartes was forced to take it on, not because he wanted the estate – he already had one, Lanhydrock in Cornwall – but because Wimpole was so heavily in hock to the Agar-Robartes Bank of which he was chairman.

Hardwicke, in other words, had effectively been repossessed by the lenders – and strangely enough by a descendant of one of Wimpole's seventeenth-century owners, Lord Radnor. Unfortunately this connection failed to endear the house to its new owners, and within five years the family had withdrawn to Lanhydrock taking with them the best of the fixtures and furniture which had come with Wimpole.

Gradually stripped in this way and let to a succession of tenants, Wimpole's salvation came in the 1930s in the shape of Mrs Bambridge. The only surviving child of Kipling and his American wife – her sister had died of pneumonia, and brother John was posted as missing presumed dead in 1915 – Elsie had had a difficult childhood with two parents who never came to terms with their double loss. In October 1924 she had married George Bambridge, a diplomat and former Irish Guards officer, and the death of her father twelve years later – at one time he had been the world's highest-paid writer – gave her the wherewithal to acquire the 2,500-acre estate and hall.

The marriage was happy but childless, and it seems reasonable to suppose that what energies might otherwise have gone into a career or raising a family were instead directed towards Wimpole and its park. For the next forty years, besides restoring the fabric of the hall, stables and other estate buildings, Elsie collected, sorted and purchased documents and other items relevant to the estate and (as she continued to do with her father's literary estate) would have copies made of those which were not available to purchase.

When she died in 1976 Wimpole Hall, the revitalised estate and the reassembled Kipling archive were willed to the National Trust. Not until 2010 was it discovered that the library included a unique proof edition of *The Jungle Book*, a precious volume complete with a personal handwritten dedication by Kipling to his daughter Josephine, Elsie's older sister who had died aged just five.

Cumbria

Lord Kitchener had his Rolls-Royce painted yellow in order that he would be recognised and given immediate priority by policemen directing traffic around the streets of London, and when the Duke of Sutherland assumed the presidency of the Royal Automobile Club in Pall Mall it was his practice to have one of his four Rolls-Royces fired up and ready to go so at all times that he could make a speedy getaway whenever he chose so to do. At the rival Automobile Association, the 5th Earl of Lonsdale (1857–1944) combined both these expensive affectations by having not just the organisation's vehicles painted yellow but literally everything else that he could get his hands on as well.

Today the AA insists the colour brings heightened visibility, a big plus when assisting members stuck on the hard shoulder in bad weather, but to his lordship it was a personal thing. More a matter of stamping his own identity on the organisation, having previously ordered a new yellow livery for his servants, had his carriages and Daimler car painted to match, and even ordered new yellow wheelbarrows and yellow cardigans for the groundsmen and foresters who worked on his estates.

For all this, 'Lordy' Lonsdale was more interested in horses than these new-fangled machines, and kept a fine stud at Barleythorpe Hall, the

Rutland estate to which he withdrew after his extravagance made it impossible to remain at his ancestral seat here at Lowther. His hunting skills were impressive – he was Master of the celebrated Cottesmore Hunt – but in the field he was never one to suffer fools.

He was known to reach for his whip if a member of the local peasantry came between him and his quarry, and on one occasion ordered a groom to shoot a favourite new hunter which had refused to jump a hedge. When the poor man declined to do so – aware that said horse was a good 'un and had cost his employer £500 – Lonsdale stood over the groom until he did as he was told.

Knowing all that, one wonders why anyone would have anything to do with him, but in 1908 the Earl laid a mammoth £21,000 wager with the millionaire banker J. Pierpont Morgan – that a man could walk around the world while supporting himself by selling postcards and finding a wife along the way.

It fell to one Harry Bensley to prove him right or wrong, but after six years and with just seven countries still to go, war broke out after the assassination at Sarajevo of Archduke Franz-Ferdinand. Bensley came home to join his local volunteers, and with Morgan dead the bet was declared void meaning his lordship hadn't lost a penny.

Derbyshire

One of the larger houses to be gifted to the nation in recent years, Calke Abbey was handed over to the National Trust barely twenty years ago when two heirs died in relatively quick succession leaving the Harpur-Crewe family facing literally crippling death duties.

The house as it is now dates back to the early eighteenth century, a baroque structure built around an Elizabethan core, the creation of an unknown architect working for Sir John Harpur, 4th Baronet on the site of an Augustinian priory rather than an abbey. For several generations the Harpurs and Harpur-Crewes played the expected part in public life, as MPs for Derbyshire constituencies and as High Sheriffs and Lord Lieutenants of the county. But then the 10th Baronet, Sir Vauncey Harpur-Crewe (1846–1924), decided he had better things to do with his time and withdrew more or less completely.

Today his reputation is as something of an altruistic autocrat, a landowner who took seriously his responsibilities towards the tenants and employees of his estate but who, as lord of the manor, fully expected to exercise some measure of control over their lives in return. In 1903 at the Market Hall in the village of Longnor, for example, he erected a 'table of tolls' giving the prices of goods to which he expected both buyers and sellers to adhere.

More positively he was known to be generous to estate workers in need, but at the same time Sir Vauncey could be cold and astonishingly aloof from both them and his own offspring. Soon servants and children alike became used to communicating with him in writing only, with notes of paternal admonishment and regulation being delivered to the daughters by one of several footmen.

Sir Vauncey it seems was something of a martinet, a great one for issuing instructions, on one occasion advising his female offspring that 'The Misses Crewe do not marry' – and making clear his very great displeasure when eventually two of them set out to prove him wrong. Even ahead of this the third of the unfortunate girls had been thrown out of the house after being seen to smoke a cigarette, and perhaps understandably she elected never to return until her father was dead.

His vehement objection to smoking had more to do with the risk to his house than to his daughter's health, a persistent worry for many owners of isolated country houses and one which may well have contributed to his decision not to equip the abbey with electricity. In fact the house had to wait until the 1960s to get this, along with the telephone. There again – and much like another rather opinionated baronet, Sir George Sitwell at Renishaw (see p. 41) – Harpur-Crewe tended to avoid any and all new-fangled technological advances, and indeed so preferred the horse to the noise, filth and smell of the motor car that the latter were banned from his estate. Bicycles too were to be left at the gate, with a carriage sent down from the abbey to collect anyone invited to visit

It has since been suggested that Sir Vauncey's dislike of the modern world came about because he had been privately educated at home instead of being sent to public school and then university – but it is equally likely that he was just a bit mad. How else to explain that, while he looked upon his estate as a near-perfect sanctuary for his beloved birds and animals – many of the dilapidated estate buildings were deliberately left unrestored to provide places for nature to thrive – the baronet spent much of his leisure time plundering it to satisfy his tastes for shooting and taxidermy? Or indeed why he should run away to the woods whenever his wife chose to entertain?

When he was not hiding in this way much of his leisure time was spent on building up his quite enormous collections of birds' eggs, moths and butterflies. Also stuffed specimens other than those shot on the estate, often rare and expensive species that he bought from dealers here and abroad. Already the Harpurs and Harpur-Crewes had a reputation for hoarding things – polished stones, toy soldiers, all kinds of curious domestic and ephemeral lumber – and this habit appeared to be reaching its apogee in Sir Vauncey.

Like many before him who are insulated from the world around them by money, rolling acres and social status, and who are able to amuse themselves by pursuing idiosyncratic interests and manias to the point of eccentricity, his collections were something Sir Vauncey gave himself to fully. Soon he had literally thousands of stuffed and mounted specimens at Calke, most of which he displayed in scores of glass cases that soon found their way into virtually every room of the house.

Of course besides being odd this sort of lifestyle is invariably costly, and an estate which is not well run soon runs up enormous bills. When Sir Vauncey died in 1924 his daughter Hilda was forced to sell some of his collection in an attempt to balance the books. By the time the estate passed to a nephew – both Sir Vauncey's sons had predeceased him – things were in an even more parlous state. Things worsened still further in 1981 when Charles Harpur-Crewe dropped dead while setting some mole traps, leading to death duties of £8 million being levied on an estate worth not an awful lot more.

The family limped on for another decade, but following another death – Henry Harpur-Crewe's, in 1991 – Calke Abbey was surrendered in lieu of taxes owed, and passed by the government of the day to the National Trust. The excitement at the time was palpable, the house described in the press as a time capsule of a place with drawers, cupboards, rooms even entire attics full of both junk and treasure which no-one seemed to have looked at – still less organised and catalogued – since the reign of Victoria.

Because of this much of it was still in absolutely mint condition, perhaps the most remarkable discovery being some early eighteenth-century silk hangings and Chinese embroidery which were found shut away in an old packing case. These were believed to have been given to a bridesmaid at the wedding of one of George II's daughters, but more than 250 years later they had still not been unwrapped. Musical instruments, book upon book of pressed dried flowers, Victorian dolls which had never been played with, an embarrassment of shooting trophies, an entire room papered from floor to ceiling with Georgian cartoons stuck straight onto the walls and in some cases three or four layers thick – the effect was to make Sir Vauncey's former home utterly beguiling but also strangely morbid. A fascinating place to visit but how wonderful to leave.

CHATSWORTH HOUSE, nr Bakewell

An engaging if personally absolutely disengaged prototype for everyone's idea of a barking mad boffin, the Hon. Henry Cavendish (1731–1810) remains all but unknown outside scientific circles despite having discovered the chemical composition of water and revealed the existence of hydrogen. He was also described by no less an authority than Sir Humphrey Davy – he of the lamp – as a great man: 'acute, sagacious, and profound, and, I think, the most accomplished British philosopher of his time.' Unfortunately, because he was somewhat backward in coming forward, he frequently left others to claim the fame for discoveries that were rightly his and his alone. Cavendish would have come to know Chatsworth in his youth but following his inheritance he chose to base himself in London, close to the learned societies.

The well-connected grandson of Chatsworth's 2nd Duke of Devonshire and the 1st Duke of Kent, and as such destined to become phenomenally rich in later life, his preference was to speak to almost no-one about anything – least of all about his scientific achievements – and he never lost the habit of thrift, perhaps as a result of being kept short by his father until he was well into middle-age.

He was known, for example, to attend Royal Society dinners with no more than 5s about his person, this being the exact cost of such a meal to the Society's Fellows. More surprisingly perhaps, he continued to follow this pattern even after coming into an inheritance of around a million pounds, a mind-boggling sum for any forty-year-old bachelor and one which would be worth probably 200 times that amount today.

Born abroad but educated at what is now Peterhouse, Cambridge, Cavendish studied mathematics for four years before turning to pneumatic chemistry and then physics. He left without graduating but thereafter corresponded frequently with the Royal Society, something he continued to do for nearly half a century. Communicating by letter was also his favoured means of dealing with his own servants, something he facilitated by equipping his two London houses (at 11 Bedford Square, Bloomsbury, and in Clapham) with a complicated system of internal mailboxes, double doors and possibly even an additional staircase in order to avoid meeting any of them or to give them an opportunity to approach him directly.

His mind, clearly, was most of the time on higher things than human intercourse and more recently it has been suggested that he suffered from Asperger's Syndrome. Unusually for such a rich man he also never showed any interest in his money or its management, and on one occasion threatened to close all his accounts when a well-meaning employee of the bank called on him to ask what to do

– in the complete absence of any instructions – with the £80,000 of interest which had accrued to him over several years. (To put that into context, the rent on a large house in Grosvenor Square, Mayfair, would at the time have been approximately £300 per annum.)

Indeed in only one regard was the Hon. Henry at all extravagant, and that was in his decision to maintain two large houses in London instead of one: the first he used as a place of work, while the other was gradually transformed into a vast library of scientific volumes and journals. Generously he allowed his fellow scientists free and easy access to the latter, although strangely he himself never borrowed so much as a pamphlet from it without first checking that it was permissible to do so – here he would always defer to his own full-time librarian – and then being sure to sign a chit to say which volumes he had taken.

It was a curious arrangement but one which in his own mind probably seemed anything but extravagant as the second house clearly served a quite separate purpose from the first. Both, it is true, were generously furnished with pictures, linen and everything else required to ensure they were equally comfortable places in which to live, but while the Bedford Square house was dedicated to knowledge already attained – hence the yards and yards of shelving filled to bursting with scientific volumes and journals – the house in Clapham celebrated the even more exciting spirit of scientific enquiry.

Piled high with scientific instruments, its purpose was to further the owner's private investigations into, among other things, the density of the Earth. To this end the house was equipped with what he termed a transit room for astronomical observations, a platform in the garden for monitoring the weather, and a fully equipped laboratory downstairs which one visitor recalls being 'stuck about with thermometers, rain gauges &tc.' Cavendish also employed a personal mathematical instrument maker at the Clapham house on a salary of £65 per annum, this in addition to the usual complement of seven indoor and outdoor staff to cope with the normal domestic requirements of a well-to-do bachelor in London.

Described by a colleague as 'shy and bashful to a degree bordering on disease', Cavendish was nevertheless not entirely reclusive all of the time. Very occasionally he entertained – guests were offered a leg of mutton every time, with nothing on the side – and as previously observed he regularly attended Royal Society dinners although at these he was, to say the least, extraordinarily ill-at-ease.

Always at great pains to ensure that he was not approached by anyone he didn't know, at the Fellows' dinners Cavendish tended to hover just outside huddles of conversation, talking to himself in precisely the kind of strange, high-pitched tone which these days would guarantee anyone a seat by himself on a train. Neither could he bear to receive praise for any of his scientific discoveries and on at least one occasion at the home of the Society's president Sir Joseph Banks he literally sprinted from the room and home to Bedford Square when someone whom he did not recognise made the mistake not just of addressing him but also of daring to look him directly in the eye.

Unsurprisingly he died alone and unmarried – prolonging life, he told his doctor, would merely be to 'prolong the misery' – whereupon he was found to be holding more bank stock than anyone in the whole of England. Nearly £1.2 million of this he left to his cousin Lord George Cavendish, and the fact that his heir spent just a tiny proportion of it (£70,000) of it acquiring a townhouse in Piccadilly – actually Burlington House, now the Royal Academy – provides some idea of the value of such inheritance at this time. Yet more of it was later spent building London's first ever shopping mall, the adjacent Burlington Arcade, but apparently only in a bid to prevent passers-by from throwing oyster shells and other unpleasant detritus over the wall and into Lord George's garden.

As for the Hon. Henry, while clearly a strange and lonely cove, it is to be hoped that he would have found some small comfort in the fact that Burlington House is now home to a number of other learned societies in addition to the RA. Today these include the Geological Society of London, the Linnaean Society of London, and – surely closer to his own heart – the Royal Astronomical Society and the Royal Society of Chemistry.

ELVASTON CASTLE, Elvaston

Is there anything more risible than an eighteenth-century dandy? Certainly not when the money begins to run out, or the looks disappear, but even without knowing the seemingly inevitable, tragic and tawdry fate of George Bryan 'Beau' Brummell it is hard to have anything but scorn for someone with such an obsession with the perfection of his own appearance. Here after all was a man who would resist lifting his hat to a lady lest he should be unable to replace it at precisely the right and most fashionable angle, and who refused to face anyone seated next to him at dinner for fear of creasing his cravat as he turned around.

Despite all this Brummell had both friends and admirers, among whom were numbered the obsessive, slightly idiotic Charles Stanhope, Viscount Petersham (1780–1851). A walking caricature of a lisping Regency Buck – the *lithp* an affectation, like almost every other aspect of his character – Lord Petersham was so concerned that his clothes should fit that he cut many of them himself, and when a boy at Eton was rumoured to be wearing whalebone stays.

The proud inventor of the 'Petersham coat', a garment which failed to catch on despite his friend the Prince Regent ordering one for every day of the week, Petersham also designed the 'Harrington hat' which met a similar fate. In addition he rarely wore anything but brown clothes and brown boots – the latter were polished using a mixture of his own invention, containing champagne – even going so far as to have elaborate cockades dyed so as to match his glazed brown hats. In the way of these things his carriage was painted a similar colour, and shortly afterwards his servants were ordered into an approximately mud-coloured livery.

In public – but rarely before dusk – he made a fetish of drinking tea (which was brown) and to take snuff at every opportunity (ditto), which he carried on his person one of his 365 snuff boxes. All needless to say were for his own personal use, and he became so particular about which one to use on what day that he was once heard to describe a French porcelain example as 'a nice summer box, but it would not do for winter wear.'

Nearly fifty when his father died (making him the 4th Earl of Harrington – hence the hat) Stanhope inherited Elvaston, a Gothic Revival house by James Wyatt. Pausing only long enough to marry an actress, many rungs beneath him socially and young enough to be his daughter, the Earl had at last something to spend time on other than apparel. In particular he wished to redesign the gardens, doing much of the design work himself after Capability Brown had rebuffed his advances.

The results were curious, to say the least, a bewildering array of Romantic English, Tuscan and Spanish styles colliding with each other in a way one visitor described as 'an outrageous phantasmagoria of artificial rock and growing wood [which] threatened to engulf the house.' The most bizarre feature was a weird folly temple which is today Elvaston's most famous attraction: a squat and rather bulbous block beneath a curved stone baldachin which saw Petersham blending Chinese, Moorish and Gothic styles in a way which, much like his hat and coat, failed entirely to catch on.

Overall, said the same unkind visitor, Elvaston was 'nowhere to lose a child after dark'. But in fact there was no danger of this as, always a monumental snob, the Earl issued regular warnings to his eighty gardeners that, 'When the Queen comes show her round, but admit no-one else.' Sadly Victoria never came and once the earl died his wife left it too, never to return. Thereafter it was a story of decline, and while there is still an Earl of Harrington, the castle now finds itself in a council-owned country park to which everyone is welcome every day especially children. The old snob would have hated it.

RENISHAW HALL, Renishaw, nr Chesterfield

Such an embarrassment that his own children took steps to avoid him, the sheer volume of ludicrous creations nevertheless means it is hard not to warm to Sir George Reresby Sitwell (1860–1943). A man who, despite a clear interest in technological progress, banned electricity from his household until well into the 1940s (and restricted guests to just two candles each) he also once expressed great disappointment at the non-appearance of a promised piece of jewellery after an acquaintance had quite clearly told him, 'I'll give you a ring on Thursday.'

Not that one would wish to spend too much time in his company, of course, since it is a measure of the man that all house guests were on arrival shown a notice requesting them 'never to contradict me in any way as it interferes with the functioning of the gastric juices and prevents my sleeping at night.' It is also probably significant that his famous offspring – the precocious and artistically inclined Osbert, Edith and Sacheverell – actually went so far as to invent a fictional yacht called the *Rover* in order that they could pretend to be sailing on it and thus avoid unnecessary visits home.

Whether or not he missed them, or believed the ruse, Sir George certainly kept himself busy. After attempting to barter for his sons' Eton College fees with pigs and potatoes grown on the estate, and stencilling Chinese willow patterns copied from plates onto his herd of cows, he would bury himself away in one of seven separate studies where he would write curious but lengthy monographs on strange subjects and experiment with a series of increasingly bizarre inventions.

Once on a visit to London he tried unsuccessfully to get the department store magnate Gordon Selfridge to stock one of the latter, the so-called Sitwell Egg being a quite disgusting-sounding confection comprising a smoked meat 'yolk', compressed-rice 'white' and a 'shell' of artificial lime. This the resourceful baronet thought would serve as the perfect portable snack for a gentleman on the move, but Selfridge thought otherwise and when Sir George was sent packing and returned to Renishaw he sensibly turned his talents to a number of non-food items.

These included a musical toothbrush which played 'Annie Laurie' while the user brushed his teeth, a unique lead-suspended mosquito net which the eighty-one-year-old insisted on using everywhere (even at home in the depths of a Derbyshire winter), and a miniature revolver which had been expressly designed for shooting wasps.

While none took off – not a single one, surprisingly – the details of each was painstakingly documented in a book entitled *My Inventions*. This was one of literally dozens he wrote while beavering away in his various studies, many of them having quite tantalising titles – *The Use of the Bed*, *Lepers' Squints*, *The History of the Fork*, *Origins of the Word Gentleman* and *Errors of Modern Parents* – although in the end Sir George failed to complete or publish a single one.

In 1925 he left Renishaw for Italy, where he had earlier purchased the ruin of the medieval Castello di Montegufoni near Florence. Here his eccentricities continued, so that visiting family members were routinely offered cold boiled water in place of wine and the land agent was repeatedly encouraged to institute methods of farming which had last been used in the fourteenth-century. Sir George was also a great traveller, and even when very old had no qualms about staying in decidedly mean digs. He always insisted on taking his butler Henry Moat along, together with a huge supply of different medicines, each bottle carefully mislabelled in order to confuse and perhaps punish anyone foolish enough to steal them.

CASTLE DROGO, Drewsteignton (NT)

The lawyer and landowner Sir Edward Coke (1552–1634) was the first to argue that an Englishman's home is his castle, and notwithstanding the fact that this former Chancellor was merely expressing a legal nicety, the reality is that deep down most of us probably wish it really was.

Sadly not many genuine castles come onto the market these days, and of those that do – isolated, damp, ruinously expensive to restore and maintain and virtually impossible to heat – most would be a nightmare to own. Of course given the wherewithal one could always build a new one, and on a somewhat modest scale the architect John Taylor is one of the few to have done it in recent years with his Castle Gryn being completed in Wales in the late 1970s.

Leaving that one aside, however, on the grounds that it is rather small, these days it is generally accepted that the last real castle to be built is the National Trust's Castle Drogo in Devon. Dreamed up by a romantically inclined department store magnate back in the 1920s it was built to a complex but engaging design by Sir Edwin Lutyens.

The early years of the twentieth century were something of a heyday for department stores and their owners, and more than a few of them spent their profits building. Gordon Selfridge bought Hengistbury Head in Dorset, and had plans for both a large and a small castle for himself, surrounded by more than 4 miles or ramparts. In London Ernest Debenham built what is still one of the most remarkable Arts and Crafts houses, its exterior covered in brilliant peacock blue, green and cream tiles and the interior a riot of Byzantine domes and details. And in Surrey there is an entire village paid for by William Whiteley, albeit posthumously after the philandering bully had been shot dead by his illegitimate son.

Another was Julius Drewe (1856–1931), a tea-buyer who made a fortune as the founder-proprietor of the Home & Colonial Stores and retired to spend it at the age of just thirty-three. Destined to lose his son and heir in the carnage at Ypres, most of the money went on building Castle Drogo which still towers over the village of Drewsteignton, Drewe having come to believe that he was a descendant of one of the Conqueror's knights, and that the knight in question, one Drogo de Teign, had owned a fortress here in the eleventh century.

In 1910, to help him along with this harmless if expensive fantasy, Drewe engaged the services of Sir Edwin Lutyens promising him the hitherto unheard of sum of £50,000 in exchange for 'a medieval fortress to match the grandeur of the site' – and to match his imagined lineage.

Sir Edwin of course was a busy man, but money talks and he began work immediately although such was the scale of the enterprise that Castle Drogo was not completed until 1931. (Unfortunately that left Mr Drewe a mere eight weeks to enjoy it, for on seeing the finished castle he had a stroke and quickly went to meet his maker, his beloved son Adrian and – who knows? – maybe even Drogo de Teign himself.)

Drewe's architect had been nothing if not thorough, however, and had even built a full-scale replica of the castle in wood and canvas so that his patron could get an idea of the finished article before work on the real thing began. When it did the results quickly proved to be as majestic as hoped, and well matched to its moorland site some 900ft above the village. With its multiple courtyards, a barbican, gatehouse, great hall and great chamber, it was also truly enormous despite the finished building eventually including just a third of the length of wall the two men had envisaged back in 1910.

Perhaps the most surprising thing about Drogo, however, was its purity. More recently it has been likened to a prison, and even a biscuit box, but Drewe bravely eschewed the usual Victorian or Edwardian approach to this kind of thing – which is to say the pursuit of the picturesque or the merely pastiche – and instead had Lutyens create a twentieth-century version of the medieval ideal. Although he later specified more than 300 electric sockets and even an advanced

vacuum-cleaning system which sucked the dust into vents set into the walls, his insistence on remaining authentic meant no pitched roofs, no drainpipes and absolutely no central heating to warm Drogo's huge granite mass.

Today, in large part because of this, the place is forbidding to say the least, and certainly a long way from being the loveliest or most comfortable of the National Trust's later properties. The views across the Teign and across Dartmoor are fantastic, and some of Lutyens' wonderful medieval detailing raises a smile, but there's a certain Dark-Age severity to the place which a real-life Drogo de Teign would have recognised.

The fenestration doesn't help either, with great stretches of wall barely broken by the castle's tiny windows, and for the modern-day visitor, particularly when numbers are low, the overwhelming sensation is one of endless stone corridors, chilly stone vaults, and a sense of seclusion. Even so, a proper castle is what Mr Drewe ordered and a proper castle is what he got.

KNIGHTSHAYES COURT, Tiverton (NT)

Drug-addicted, destined to die early and physically so unprepossessing that even friends called him ugly, William Burges (1827–81) is nevertheless to be counted among the greatest of Victorian architects and designers even though his personal brand of romantic medievalism always stood at odds to the industrial and technological triumphs of that age.

His professional career was short, with a mere eighteen years elapsing between his first major commission and his death from a chill which he caught in Cardiff. He was down there working for his favourite patron, the 3rd Marquess of Bute, who was quite possibly the richest man in Britain and on whose behalf Burges was retained to rebuild Cardiff Castle and reconstruct another around the ruins of the thirteenth-century Castell Coch.

Lord Bute's enormous income from a combination of industry and inheritance was a crucial factor in the success of their relationship, chiefly because Burges – short, fat and so goggle-eyed as to once mistake a peacock for a friend, or possibly a friend for a peacock – sincerely believed that 'good art is far too rare and far too precious ever to be cheap' and priced his services accordingly.

All of which makes one wonder how it was that Sir John Heathcoat-Amory came to employ him in the first place. A family of farmers and inventors, the Heathcoats (as they then were) had relocated from Derbyshire to Devon after a gang of Luddites had smashed up their inventions. They were not exactly poor – towards the end of the nineteenth-century their lace-making factory was the biggest in the world – but Sir John was still really only a country gentleman and clearly nowhere near as rich as an authentic territorial magnate like Lord Bute.

He must also surely have known something of the reputation that Burges had for extravagance, which in his own lifetime was becoming legendary. And what of the still somewhat vexing question of why such a straight-laced huntin' and shootin' country gent would have wanted to have any dealings with a slightly wacky opium-addicted bachelor who liked to go rat-catching in his leisure time? Or to have taken on a man who had expressed his determination to create 'a medieval fairyland'?

Burges was also well known for his opinion that all the houses he had ever created were created for him – surely a warning to any client – and that money was only ever a 'secondary consideration' because 'there are no bargains in art'. Heathcoat-Amory took him on nevertheless, but very soon found himself looking at the foundations of a house far bigger than he could afford – work on an immense tower at the western end was halted when only the base had been completed – and certainly much bigger than he could afford to decorate using someone as keen as Burges was on interior decoration, and as expensive.

His solution was simple enough though: he sacked William Burges and brought in the rather cheaper John Dibblee Crace whose father had been in partnership with A.W. Pugin. Crace managed to complete the house more or less on time and on budget, and produced something closer to what Sir John was after. It was, even so, Burges who was to have the last laugh when it came to Knightshayes Court, although it was to take another 100 years for the full story to unfold.

The reality was that by the time the house was completed, the heyday of Victorian taste was well and truly over, and for the next century interest in Victoriana, Crace's contribution to it (and William Burges for that matter) could not have been more diminished. The novelist Evelyn Waugh had a much-prized Burges washstand – it was he who observed how it is that the British appreciate their cultural heritage only after it is gone – but very few others cared for the style of Knightshayes Court and its ilk. By the time Burges died in 1881 owners and occupiers of such houses – including Sir John's descendants – were already taking steps to rid their homes of any traces of the Gothic

Revival, dismantling entire rooms or covering them over, and looking for something else altogether.

Thereafter the reversal was an exceptionally long time in coming, and it was not until the 1980s – by which time the National Trust had taken over the house – that people really began to appreciate the work of the Revivalists. When they did it was the name of William Burges which sprang to the fore, not Crace's, and seeking to restore Knightshayes the Trust looked to his work rather than to that of his contemporaries. Furniture was brought to Devon from the Tower House in London (another Burges design, now owned by the Led Zeppelin guitarist Jimmy Page) and from Oxford came a fireplace installed by Burges when he had redecorated the Worcester College in the 1860s.

Today, as a result, Knightshayes Court is very much a Burges House, which is to say not Sir John Heathcote-Amory's, nor really the National Trust's either, and certainly not John Dibblee Crace's.

Dorset

At best an enigmatic and confusing character, Thomas Edward Lawrence CB, DSO (1888–1935) combined a thirst for self-publicity with desire to be left alone, also a hatred of being touched although a masochistic streak meant he liked a friend to beat him with a cane. He also displayed an extraordinary extravagance when it came to boys' toys, and one which still sits uneasily with the otherwise ascetic lifestyle he claimed to be seeking when he rented this small former workman's cottage in Devon.

The illegitimate son of an Anglo-Irish baronet who absconded with his daughters' governess, Lawrence's passions for travel and archaeology took him to the Middle East after a period spent studying history at Oxford. (He also claimed to have served as a boy soldier with the Royal Artillery, although no documentation has come to light to confirm this.) In danger of 'going native' while digging in Syria, Lawrence began to identify strongly with the nomadic desert Arabs and quickly learned to speak Arabic. Both were attributes which proved extremely useful when war broke out with Germany, and ones he was able to put to good use when encouraging the locals to rise against Ottoman Empire forces fighting on the side of the Kaiser.

Though short, Lawrence's skill, panache and courage were never in any doubt. He was injured at least sixty times but fighting alongside Arab irregulars he and his men, using three converted Rolls-Royce Silver Ghosts, could soon claim to have obliterated a couple of enemy command posts, blown up a bridge, wiped out almost an entire regiment of enemy cavalry and repeatedly destroyed stretches of the strategically important Hejaz Railway. Invariably heavily outnumbered, Lawrence called this 'fighting de-luxe', confidently asserting that 'all the Turks in Arabia could not fight a single Rolls-Royce armoured car in open country. They were worth hundreds of men to us in these deserts.'

Recognising their strength and incredible durability, the idea of using Silver Ghosts as the basis of fighting machines had come from Bendor, 2nd Duke of Westminster, who promptly donated a dozen such cars from his estate in Cheshire. Soon other rich and titled owners were handing over their own cars to be converted to military specification, among them Lord Rothschild who later proved Lawrence's claim that it was 'almost impossible to break a Rolls-Royce'

when he was forced to wield a sledge-hammer in order to prevent his own from falling into enemy hands.

The dashing spectacle of chaps engaging the enemy in such style naturally caught the public's imagination on both sides of the Atlantic, and after cooperating with the American war correspondent and film-maker Lowell Thomas, Lawrence was soon dubbed 'of Arabia' and found himself an international celebrity. He cheerfully contributed to his own legend, by publishing a best-selling memoir (*The Seven Pillars of Wisdom*, which he was forced to rewrite after leaving the first 250,000 words behind on a train) but, having done so, promptly decided he was uneasy with the fame and attempted to slip away unnoticed.

In 1922 he sought to escape his celebrity by buying a plot of land in Epping Forest, and building himself a simple hut in the woods where he could swim in peace and read. When that did not work he resigned his commission, Lt-Col. Lawrence hastily reinventing himself as 'Aircraftman Ross' and joining the rank and file of the RAF. He later transferred to the Royal Tank Corps when his cover was blown by the *Daily Express*, enlisting as a private and renaming himself again as 'T.E. Shaw'. Later still he decided he preferred the RAF after all, which eventually he was permitted to rejoin.

In 1925, while stationed with the RTC at Bovingdon Camp in Dorset, Lawrence rented and then purchased a small cottage nearby called Clouds Hill. By 1935 he was living in it full-time, a more comfortable proposition than his hut in Chingford but still a tiny place and decidedly spartan. His apparent asceticism extended only so far, however, and as well as entertaining widely at Clouds Hill – although he himself was a teetoal non-smoker – Lawrence treated himself to some flashy diversions. These included a new speedboat – no stranger to water, during his time with the RAF he had been involved with the Schneider Trophy race for seaplanes – and a succession of enormously fast Brough Superior motorcycles for which he built a rather twee thatched garage.

Dubbed the 'Rolls-Royce of motorcycles' until the famous car manufacturer stepped in to object when George Brough diversified into car production, these were very superior machines indeed. One of them might easily have cost more than Clouds Hill to buy, yet Lawrence bought seven in succession, referring to them as Boas (short for 'Boanerges', meaning 'sons of thunder') and naming each one George with individual numbering from I through to VII.

George VIII was on order from the factory in Nottingham and nearing completion when, on an early summer's day in 1935, Lawrence went over the handlebars after executing an uncontrolled swerve to avoid two cyclists. The precise cause of the accident has never really been identified, but years later – after Lawrence had slipped into a coma and died – enthusiasts for the marque were still quick to point out how well the bike stood up to the crash and how little damage it sustained when the rider lost control.

A year after the accident Lawrence's brother, A.W. Lawrence, a professor of classical archaeology at Cambridge University, gave Clouds Hill to the National Trust. With it came a 1930s sleeping bag – unfortunately this was later stolen – which had at different times been used by the poet Robert Graves, E.M. Forster and another Brough rider, George Bernard Shaw.

ST GILES HOUSE, Wimborne St Giles

Most visitors to London know the statue of Eros in Piccadilly Circus, but few know much about the figure itself or how it came to be. Strictly speaking it is not the pagan god of love at all, but rather the 'Angel of Christian Charity' which was erected at the end of Shaftesbury Avenue to commemorate the life and achievements of the Victorian philanthropist and leading anti-slavery campaigner Anthony Ashley Cooper (1801–85).

Cooper was more formally the 7th Earl of Shaftesbury, something the sculptor acknowledged by having his figure of an archer aiming downwards in order to *bury* the *shaft* of his arrow. In a similar fashion he also noted the Cooper family's ancient Dorset origins by deliberately aligning the archer's arrow towards Wimborne St Giles and the Shaftesburys' seat at St Giles House on an estate they had owned since the 1460s.

Shaftesbury's work to improve the lot of slaves, factory workers, chimney-sweeps and others was doubtless impressive but his passion for helping unfortunates meant he was occasionally caricatured, especially after he agreed to meet with forty convicted felons so that he could offer them some helpful advice about switching to another career.

He was also an early pioneer of Christian Zionism, somewhat eccentrically for a man of his time and background believing that the restoration of the Jews to the Holy Land – and in time the establishment of a new state of Israel – was something entirely in accordance with Biblical prophecies.

This ought to have made him a friend of the Jewish people, and indeed might have done but for his presidency for more than thirty-five years of the Society for Promoting Christianity Among the Jews. Unfortunately this made one thing abundantly clear: far from being interested in what was good for the Jews, Cooper was far more interested in converting Jews to Anglicanism and then shipping them off to the Middle East.

He was cunning about it too, recruiting countless leading politicians, bishops and even the Archbishops of Canterbury and York to his cause, but all the while concealing his religious theories. Instead of talk of Biblical prophecies he concentrated on the material benefits which would accrue to the Empire – and more particularly to Palmerston's government – if and when the Middle East were to be 'stabilised' by the settling of hundreds of thousands of new migrants overseen by a British consul in Jerusalem.

Shaftesbury, in fact, had little if anything good to say about Judaism itself, and apparently no regard for this most ancient religion or the sophisticated culture that had grown up around it. Not that he was an anti-Semite exactly, which at this time would have been far from eccentric, but rather he saw Jews as somewhat odd and archaic throwbacks. Without pausing for a moment to ask whether they might have their own views about what was right for them and what was not, he just pressed on regardless and was convinced, like so many vocal social reformers then and now, that He Knew Best.

On the surface the organisation under his long presidency looked triumphant. The great and the good of British society were numbered among its patrons and supporters. The administration was exceptionally richly endowed and splendidly accommodated in several countries. Its premises included schools for the young and meeting places where teas were hosted for the older ones. Bible classes were run for all ages, and over the years the Society gave out free copies of the New Testament to anyone who wanted one – but thousands more to people who didn't but couldn't bring themselves to say so.

Unfortunately what it really lacked was an audience, a constituency, and despite the efforts of Shaftesbury and his cohorts this significant shortfall was something the Society never really overcame. There was the odd convert, such as the Polish Rabbi Ginsberg who was reborn as the somewhat unlikely sounding the Revd Crichton-Ginsberg before being sent out as a missionary. In one year (1862) he managed to recruit a total of three Jews to Christ's cause, but that was a good year and such heady success was never to be repeated. Thereafter it took one of his colleagues twenty-three years to match Crichton-Ginsberg's meagre total, while the best that could be said of the Society's other missionaries was that the copies of the New Testament they gave away were 'rarely burnt or torn up as it was some years ago.'

Eventually, happily, the Society for Promoting Christianity Among the Jews crumbled and today it must be counted as one of the great reformer's few failures. Not many others saw it that way, however, with Shaftesbury's own father at one point commissioning a book to denounce the organisation, and other observers accepting that whatever the Earl's motives may have been the idea was hopeless, even idiotic, and always bound to fail.

Whether Shaftesbury himself ever recognised this isn't known, and it seems unlikely. Just once he might have glimpsed how others saw his crusade, however, which was when the incorrigible do-gooder agreed to chair the Lunacy Commission. In that role he was shown round an asylum and when introduced to one of the inmates asked how it was known she was mad. The reason given was simple and to the point: she subscribed to an organisation which wanted to make Christians out of Jews – hence the diagnosis.

Essex

Thomas Barrett-Lennard (1826–1918) took an MA at Peterhouse, Cambridge, succeeded to his grandfather's baronetcy at the age of thirty-one, and as a traditional local Victorian grandee held the office of High Sheriff of Essex while sitting as chairman of the local Asylums Committee, giving him a watching brief over the care meted out to local loons.

In his spare time what interested him most, however, were animals which he held in the highest esteem. His fondness for four-legged creatures extended not just to the usual retinue of horses, hounds and pointers which would have been found around any English country home at this time, but also to the many rats which ran in the fields and invaded the barns of Belhus, his gloriously gothick Essex estate.

When their time was up, the family horses, dogs and cats were buried in special plots in the grounds, these sort of private pet cemeteries being commonplace on big estates in the years before the First World War. (London has one too, built in the environs of Kensington Palace and visible from the Bayswater Road.) Sir Thomas took things a good deal further than most, however, demanding not only that the vicar from nearby Aveley officiate at the proceedings but also that his own footmen attend each animal funeral in full livery and take the weight of the animals' caskets which he had purpose-made for the occasion.

Whether the rats got the same treatment at Belhus is not recorded, although they certainly had a better time than most, the squire insisting that his outdoor staff ensure that bowls of fresh water were provided in the hay barns for them to drink from, and expressly forbidding any of his servants to kill or injure rodents found within the house or grounds.

The result, unsurprisingly, was that the rats thrived and (like those living in the First World War trenches) soon grew to enormous size. As one housemaid later put it, 'they were as big as cats, and as tame as tame could be. The noise they made was like people running up and down the corridor. Sometimes you could hear chairs moving – they were everywhere.'

Sir Thomas was fond of rooks too, while the deer at Belhus were guaranteed never to be made into venison. Similarly, while he happily provided kennels for the South Essex Foxhounds, he refused to ride with them and sooner than killing foxes would go steeplechasing instead. On the other hand, while he was kind enough to open his own front door so as to save his servants the bother, as an old man (he died aged ninety-two) he once administered what the local newspaper described as 'a tremendous hiding' to a tradesman whom he had caught mistreating a pony.

A shabby dresser who on more than one occasion was mistaken for his own gatekeeper and tipped a shilling, in later life Sir Thomas was arrested on his way home from a meeting at Brentwood of the Essex Asylum Committee. After being spotted emerging from a hedge – presumably he was taking a short-cut back to Belhus – he was mistaken for an escapee rather than one of the asylum's honoured guests.

Sir Thomas died in 1918, leaving Belhus to his son (also called Thomas). With no children, and another estate in Norfolk which he preferred, the new Sir Thomas had no desire to move south and Belhus remained only intermittently occupied until it was requisitioned by the Army at the start of the Second World War.

Already a good part of the estate had been compulsorily purchased as building land, and by the war's end the house had been bombed as well as being trashed by the troops billeted there. The family neither seemed to want it back nor could afford to restore it, and like so many English country houses it was torn down in the 1950s and the site grassed over. Today the outline of its foundations can still be paced out on a local golf course, although the sad likelihood is that wild animals are less welcome on the greens and in the bunkers than they were back in the day of batty Sir Thomas.

CHAMPION LODGE, nr Maldon

Joining the Royal Navy at age thirteen, and transferring to the King's Royal Rifle Corps five years later, the young Claude Champion de Crespigny (1847–1935) just couldn't wait to get stuck in. Unsurprisingly he had little time for office types, particularly any of those pencil-necked bureaucrats who seemed determined to come between him and his rock solid conviction that 'where there is a daring deed to be done, and in any part of the world, an Englishman should leap to the front to accomplish it.'

Fighting he felt was the only true indicator of character – a properly manly occupation – and in the absence of a good war to fight (and genuinely sorry that duelling to the death was no longer legal) he frequently offered a thrashing to anyone he felt deserved it. For a man of honour such as himself, his obituary in *The Times* was later to note, nothing else came close to a duel and if guns, swords and knives were forbidden then fists would just have to do when it came to sorting out a difference between two parties.

Always keen to extend the privilege of combat to the lower orders during an unwelcome lull in international hostilities, on inheriting a baronetcy the new Sir Claude Champion De Crespigny decided to institute a new rule at his home, the aptly named Champion Lodge at Heybridge in Essex. From now on, he insisted, no men would be taken on to the staff before first going a few rounds with their would-be employer. Win or lose, he said, they would get the job providing they had showed sufficient spirit.

Tramps in the vicinity of the estate would similarly be offered the chance to box him for a hot dinner, and to his credit Sir Claude kept up his end of the bargain even when some chums organised a 'ringer' by paying a professional pugilist to dress as a tramp and position himself by one of the gate lodges. Before long, as expected, Sir Claude duly appeared at the gate, took one look at the fellow, threw down the challenge – and took a beating. Fortunately he afterwards saw the funny side of this, and having proved himself the boxer was invited up to the lodge for tea.

Always looking out for a new challenge of one sort of another, in 1869 Sir Claude must been extremely disappointed when Henry Morton Stanley turned down the Englishman's offer to accompany him on his expedition to locate Dr Livingstone. (Stanley did so on the eminently sensible grounds that he, Sir Claude, had no actual experience of the dark continent. Not that this was de Crespigny's fault, you understand, but for a number of reasons he had as he put it been unable 'to take part as a volunteer in several of our little African wars.')

The tightrope-walker Blondin similarly refused him permission to have a go on the wire stretched tightly across Niagara Falls, and while in 1889 he succeeded in being posted to Egypt to cover some Dervish-inspired unpleasantness (for the *Sporting Times*, bizarrely) his hopes were dashed again when the authorities refused to accept that he was a genuine war correspondent or indeed that such a newspaper would even employ one. In the end he never made it to the front, nor into the thick of the Boer War a few years later.

His postings to India and Ireland were slightly more successful, however, and as well as proving himself a first-class steeplechaser, Sir Claude undertook a number of daredevil challenges clearly intended to give him the endorphin rush he so badly needed. In 1883 he and a colleague became the first men ever to fly a balloon across the North Sea, and then at the age of forty-two – despite having broken more than a dozen bones – he succeeded in swimming the Nile Rapids which no European had previously managed to do. Convinced he had discovered something of value here, and naturally keen that his children should also be good swimmers, he taught them how to do it using a method of his own devising which involved pushing the youngsters off a boat and leaving them to work out how to swim to safety.

Thereafter (none of them having drowned) Sir Claude was acknowledged as a sportsman of great ability, with even the *New York Times* identifying him as someone able to 'hunt like a hound, swim like a fish, run like a hare and box like [James J.] Jeffries.' Unfortunately he had a darker side to him too, and it subsequently emerged that Sir Claude had worked occasionally as a volunteer hangman in Carlisle, a hobby he preferred to keep to himself by hiding behind the *nom de noose*, Charles Maldon.

HEDINGHAM CASTLE, Castle Hedingham

In the interests of fairness it should perhaps be said that, unlike others in this book who on the whole have only themselves to blame, Edward de Vere, 17th Earl of Oxford (1550–1604) had eccentricity thrust upon him and only long after he himself had passed on.

The prime mover in this was one J. Thomas Looney, a north country teacher who, after losing his faith while training for the priesthood, developed an interest in William Shakespeare which in 1920 led him to question whether the so-called Bard of Stratford had in fact written any of the works commonly ascribed to him.

On balance Looney thought it unlikely that he had, adopting what is now referred to as his anti-Stratfordian stance on the basis of similarities he noted between de Vere's life (and to a lesser degree his literary techniques) and the contents of Shakespeare's most famous plays and sonnets.

In truth de Vere – any de Vere – might at first have looked like an odd candidate for a litterateur. Previous earls of Oxford had been of a decidedly martial character, a dynasty of crusader knights riding out from their own mighty Norman fortress – Hedingham Castle remained the family's seat for more than 400 years – holding numerous great offices of state and notching up an impressive series of battle honours including both Crècy and Agincourt.

There is, too, plenty of evidence that the 17th Earl was cut from much the same cloth, a leading light at court who (fully prepared to honour the military might of his forebears when the call came in 1588) lost no time in collecting his 'armour and furniture' and racing to the coast to repel the Armada of Phillip II.

That said, de Vere also found plenty of time for gentler, more artistic pursuits, taking a lease on London's celebrated Blackfriars Theatre – in which, years later, Shakespeare was a shareholder – and exercising such a generous patronage over friends in the literary and dramatic worlds that in his own lifetime more than two dozen books were dedicated to him by the leading writers of his day.

The Earl also published a small body of his own work, including eight poems, *The Paradise of Dainty Devises* (1576), a collection since recognised as having created 'a dramatic break with everything known to have been written at the Elizabethan court up to that time.' He gained similar plaudits, with one leading critic, George Puttenham, being numbered among a crew of literary-minded courtiers who 'have written excellently and would appear if their doings could be found out and made publicke with the rest, of which number is first that noble Gentleman Edward Earle of Oxford.'

Much of Looney's thesis, however, depends not so much on de Vere's output as on his own lifestyle and prodigious learning. In particular he contrasts Shakespeare's modest upbringing and poor education with the richness and worldliness of those plays and sonnets he is supposed to have written, works which encompass the sort of people and places the Earl would have known well and recognised. By contemporary standards de Vere was a highly skilled linguist, exceptionally well-travelled and exceptionally well-read, and certainly his experiences as a sophisticate, socialite and courtier would likely have given him far more insight into the human condition than those of a provincial nobody such as William Shakespeare.

Looney claimed also to have detected a marked shift in the tenor and tone of those plays published after 1604 (the year that de Vere died), suggesting that *The Tempest* and *Pericles, Prince of Tyre*, were the work of a third hand, perhaps brought in to adapt or complete material his lordship had not had time to finish.

Unfortunately such ideas, while intriguing, found little favour then among the majority of literature professors and Shakespearean scholars, and nor do they now. It is interesting to note, however, that Looney did have some singularly impressive supporters – including Sigmund Freud – and that nearly seventy years after his own death (and more than 400 after de Vere's) the Shakespearean mainstream is still forced to acknowledge the Oxfordian argument and is still working hard to discredit it.

Gloucestershire

SNOWSHILL MANOR, Snowshill, nr Broadway (NT)

Located in the Cotswold village of the same name, the manor dates back to the early sixteenth century but is very much the creation of Suffolk-born Charles Paget Wade (1883–1956). Wade was an associate of the socially-minded architectural practice of Parker and Unwin, prime movers in the vernacular and Arts and Crafts movements, although these days he is remembered more for his huge and diverse collections than for his professional career.

Wade had first spotted an advertisement for the manor in an old copy of *Country Life* which somehow found its way to the Western Front where he was doing his bit for the Army in the First World War. It was still for sale in 1919 and having inherited a fortune built on the West Indian sugar trade he was well placed to make an offer. The offer was accepted, although on inspection the house on its steep hillside turned out to be extremely run-down and almost hidden from sight behind a jungle of nettles and giant thistles.

It was nevertheless absolutely what Wade had been looking for: a huge project which was to require a good deal of skill and sensitivity as well as substantial funding. At this stage the house lacked all modern conveniences, and while retaining as much of the original stonework and wooden panelling as possible, Wade took the decidedly eccentric decision to eschew such recent contrivances as electricity and incandescent light bulbs (in favour of the softer, more friendly glow of candles and oil lamps) while he and Mackay Baillie-Scott set to remodelling the surrounding gardens in their favoured Arts and Crafts style.

Equally eccentric was his decision not to live at the manor, but instead to withdraw to what had been a tiny priest's lodging in the grounds before its subsequent conversion to a bakehouse. Its religious origins were something Wade very much valued, and in later life – he was a great one for dressing up and owned 2,000 costumes – he liked to materialise silently from one of its dark corners in the hope of spooking friends such as John Betjeman, Virginia Woolf and Graham Greene. When entertaining or dining alone, a pair of bread ovens provided the only means of cooking and staying warm – although more often than not women in the village (worried that Wade might starve) provided him with a sort of upmarket meals-on-wheels.

The manor meanwhile was set aside to house his collections, an agglomeration of nearly 30,000 objects which he had been amassing since being shown a Chinese cabinet full of an aunt's curios while a lonely child of only seven.

Including everything from poison bottles to prams, tools to telescopes, sundials to the largest collection of Samurai armour outside Japan, the collections still fill every square inch of the house and its outbuildings, and are crammed into every available space from the ground floor to the commodious attics. Occasionally the rooms' names seem to provide a tantalising if slight inkling as to their contents – 'Dragon', 'Meridian', 'Top Gallant', 'Zenith' and 'Seraphim' – but any attempt at categorisation soon breaks down when anyone tries to get a handle on what drove Wade's passion for acquisition.

In fact the clue lies in craftsmanship – he was a designer and woodworker as well as an architect – and the vast majority of his possessions, while some of it is now rare and valuable, attracted Charles Wade primarily he said because they provided such a good record of many fast-disappearing crafts and skills.

Put like that his aim sounds admirable, and so it was, although the overall effect is often to say more about the owner of the house than the contents. A worryingly high proportion are children's toys but most obviously the sheer quantity of items suggests something of an obsession if not a mania, and a majority of visitors to Snowshill these days are scarcely able to take in the immense range of stuff and lumber Wade collected let alone to make any headway when it comes to appreciating its detail and quality. Some of it is anyway just junk, although making one's way through the myriad passages and beneath barrel-vaulted ceilings it would take a hard-hearted visitor to point this out.

Full of surprises Wade suddenly married at sixty-three – prior to this he had shown little if any interest in such a thing – although Mrs Wade preferred the sun to Snowshill and spent most of their marriage in the West Indies. Before deciding to join her there in 1951 he gifted his home and its contents to the National Trust, but it was to be decades before that organisation finally discovered just how much they were taking on. It seemed that even Wade had underestimated the number of objects by more than 8,000, and when it came to restoring Snowshill Manor a few years ago an incredible twenty-three trucks had to be used to haul away literally hundreds of packing cases just so the builders could come in.

With everything now back in place it still feels absolutely like his house, and of course it still is. Not just because it provided some compensation for his lonely, unhappy childhood – which doubtless it did – but also because, more than half a century after he walked out of Snowshill Manor for the last time, Trust staff still like to think his ghost lingers in the inky shadows, and that Charles Paget Wade is still keeping an eye on his extraordinary creation.

Hertfordshire

Contemptuous of his family and dismissive of its elaborately gothick seat at Ashridge, as a commoner Francis Henry Egerton (1756–1829) fell out badly with the 7th Earl of Bridgewater (his brother) and expressed himself grossly disappointed in the Duke (his uncle). He was nevertheless in thrall to the Bridgewaters' well-documented history and ducal status, and when he came into the lesser title (together with an income of £40,000 a year) the new 8th Earl of Bridgewater lost no time in applying the family arms to literally everything that he possibly could.

Preferring France to England he took off for Paris, but never much one for Parisian society (he spoke better Latin than French) the unmarried peer spent more time in the company of animals than humans – in particular his cats and dogs whom he furnished with silver collars bearing the family crest. His favourites were said to be two dogs named Bijou and Biche, and before long he had adopted the habit of taking meals with them – or rather, they would sit down with him – in preference to members of his own species.

Insisting his animals were always well turned out – he had boots and gowns made for them by the best makers of the day – Lord Bridgewater also required his pets to display the best possible manners once his footmen had tied linen napkins around their necks and put their monogrammed plates before them. Those which refused to were consigned to servants' hall for a week, a sentence he clearly felt to be rather harsh and probably more than most well brought up dogs would be able to bear.

On the rare occasions when a human was invited to join his Paris table, Lord Bridgewater's guests were offered nothing more inviting than plain boiled beef, this even though his modest city garden was crammed to the walls with 300 rabbits, 300 pigeons and 300 partridges which were specially ordered in so that Lord Bridgewater could take pot-shots at them whenever the yearning for a little sport overcame him.

His dogs were also allowed to accompany him on his rides around Paris, the impressively liveried Bridgewater coach becoming a familiar sight around the streets of the city where it was instantly recognisable not just by the crests on the doors, but also by the silk cushions provided

for the comfort of up to half a dozen canines at a time. Umbrella-wielding footmen were also on hand so that the dogs could shelter while relieving themselves in the Bois du Boulogne.

While reportedly something of a slob when it came to his own table-manners, the dogs' master was nevertheless always immaculately apparelled and is believed never to have worn an item more than once. He also required his valet to keep and catalogue all his cast-offs in the order in which he had worn them. This perhaps explains why, when the crazy English milord went travelling, he required a caravan of sixteen carriages for his personal effects, and thirty servants to ensure that his daily routine never waivered from plan. It also enabled him to tell what day it was by looking at his clothes, and counting back.

Curiously, when he died none of his animals received so much as a mention in his will; instead the aforementioned servants were each issued with a suit of mourning clothes, a cocked hat and three pairs of stockings and instructed to keep his household running for a further two months as if their master was still alive. The money itself he left to charity – including a mammoth £8,000 to the author or authors of the best work on 'the Goodness of God as manifested in the Creation' – presumably because by then he had no longer any contact with his family and absolutely no-one he could call a friend. Glorious, eccentric Ashridge itself is now a business school, with the estate part of the National Trust.

HATFIELD HOUSE, nr Hatfield

A rare lady among the lords when it comes to eccentrics, the 1st Marchioness of Salisbury (1750–1835) was always very much her own woman, and at a time when many of the wives of great men spent their days sitting around behind gently fluttering fans, Lady Salisbury kept herself busy, as one guest at Hatfield House put it, by doing 'anything and everything all day long'.

A keen hunter, in the absence of an accepted form of dress for women she designed her own outfit comprising a coat in the Salisbury colours of blue and silver and a small black jockey's cap. She also took on the responsibilities of master when the 1st Marquess decided he had had enough, and kept at it until her eighties by which time she was so frail she had to be strapped onto the horse and so blind that she needed to be told when to jump by a groom galloping alongside.

Deeply distrustful of organised religion, she avoided going to church, was frequently observed playing cards for money on the Sabbath, and when summoned to Westminster Abbey to hear the music of Mr Handel made such a commotion during the recital that George III demanded to know what was going on. On being told it was Lady Salisbury, clearly a repeat offender, he is reported to have dropped the subject immediately.

A keen if reckless gambler who made frequent trips to the capital where she would play all night, Lady Salisbury was also something of a show-off and took care always to dress in a conspicuously grand fashion. Always mindful of her rank – and expecting others to defer to her at every opportunity – she was nevertheless quite irrationally generous with the lower orders, and when in a playful mood liked to fling golden guineas from her carriage while travelling around her husband's estate.

As was only to be expected she refused to grow old gracefully, and certainly never accepted her diminished role as dowager when the death of her husband meant the estate should pass to her son, his two wives and eleven children. By this time she was well into her seventies but chose to adopt a style of dress more suited to a young girl – all whites, pale yellows, gigantic bows and bonnets – while refusing even to consider surrendering the family jewels and decorations which by rights should have been handed on to the new Marquess.

These days we would describe the look she was after as mutton dressed as lamb, but one contemporary observer offered a more detailed description when he noted how it 'is impossible to do justice to the antiquity of her face. If, as alleged, she is only 74 years-old, it is the most cracked or rather furrowed piece of mosaic you have ever saw.'

By eighty-five Lady Salisbury had returned to another fashion from her far distant youth, of wearing her hair piled up high and stuck through with feathers, and it is this affectation which finally brought about her end in November 1835. We cannot know for sure, but it is assumed one of the feathers drifted free and caught fire while she was writing letters by the light of a candle, and with a strong wind whipping up the flames the 1st Marchioness of Salisbury was soon burned to a crisp in the ensuing conflagration.

Ordinarily, though tragic, this might have been something of a relief – the Dowager's extravagance was becoming an intolerable drain on the estate – but unfortunately she took with her most of the west wing thereby bequeathing her son an altogether different kind of fiscal nightmare. Also lost to the flames were the fabulous Salisbury jewels – or so it was thought until, raking through the ashes, it became apparent that these were only copies and that the originals had long since been sold to pay off what had clearly been some of the old lady's very substantial gambling debts.

LETCHWORTH HALL, nr Letchworth

Now substantially extended as part of an hotel, the seventeenth-century manor house known as Letchworth Hall was left to the Revd John Alington (1795–1863) together with more than forty farms in the area and a fortune not far short of a million pounds.

Unsurprisingly it went to his head, and after picking a quarrel with the local vicar – for which he was suspended by the Bishop of St Albans – the previously mild-mannered, Westminster and Balliol-educated vicar established what was virtually his own new religion, with rival communions being held at the hall in competition with the official ones at the parish church of St Mary's.

The battle between the two was always going to be unequal from the start, and not just because so many of the villagers were workers on the Letchworth Hall estate (or tenant farmers) that a majority of parishioners would have felt obliged to side with their lord of the manor. Their numbers were additionally boosted by a general invitation which went out to travellers, tramps and gypsies, and by the fact the sermons were frequently given on risqué topics – free love was a favourite, with quotations from the *Song of Solomon* – and would be followed by a distribution of free beer and brandy to the congregation.

Eventually, inevitably, the proceedings would get out of hand, with the amorous being advised by their vicar to continue outside on the grass, and a shotgun being bandied about from one of the two pulpits he had built at the hall to deter others in the pews from brawling. The Revd Alington was also a bit of a showman, sporting a leopard skin vestment of his own design and Moroccan slippers, and travelling up the aisle at high speed on a dandy-horse (an early type of bicycle) which was propelled by a couple of servants.

After this grand entrance the service would typically commence with a little music – nothing sacred, you understand, but the product of two clockwork musical boxes and an old piano nicknamed 'Tidlee Bump' – after which the celebrant, almost certainly inebriated, would flit from one pulpit to the other and back again while reading out love poems interspersed with amorous little narratives from various questionable sources.

Attendance at St Mary's naturally plummeted, together with the revenue from the collection plate which was soon hardly worth sending round. The Revd Hartopp Knapp also found his own income badly hit when Alington, flush with his considerable inheritance, decided to cut agricultural production on the estate thus reducing the tithe payable to the church. Always a generous landlord, however, he was at pains to ensure that the farmworkers did not suffer as a consequence and in the absence of any real work would pay them to carry out invented tasks such as excavating and then filling in large holes in the otherwise barren fields.

In 1851 he also took all the estate workers on a paid-for jolly to the Great Exhibition, having first taught them the route from King's Cross station to the Crystal Palace using a scale model of the relevant parts of London which he had created on the estate using fallen tree trunks to represent the layout of the streets. Needless to say this did little more than confuse everybody, and a number of yokels were reportedly lost for several days. A few years later the trunks were brought out again, to create a scale representation of various skirmishes in the Crimean War, but with no more success.

In 1858 the Revd Knapp threw in the towel and moved away, after which Alington held a service of thanks. Now in his sixties, the old man soldiered on for a few more years but then sickened in the winter of 1863. Taking to his bed, and finding the prescribed medicine too disgusting to swallow, he called for a large glass of brandy, drank it, sighed loudly and slipped away. A couple of days later the 'Mad vicar of Old Letchworth' was interred in the local churchyard, buried in a coffin he had purchased some years before and in which he had liked to be carried around his garden in what he called a practice run for the 'real thing'.

The Letchworth Hall Hotel still sports the curious battlemented tower which Alington added to it on coming into his inheritance, as well as an Allington Wing [*sic*] and a Great Hall complete with minstrels' gallery which is where many of Alington's unorthodox services are believed to have taken place.

LOCKLEYS, nr Welwyn Garden City

An intelligent, highly inventive but worryingly obsessive oddball in the finest traditions of the English eccentric, George Edward Dering FRS (1831–1911) had both the time and space needed for the effective pursuit of technological progress thanks to an inheritance from his mother's side of not one but two large estates, one each on either side of the Irish Sea.

As the very picture of a crusty old bachelor, Dering only ever worked alone on his inventions, and seemed very much to prefer the fourteenth-century Lockleys estate to his one in County Galway. He was, even so, absent from it for up to a year at a time, but still insisted the staff have mutton chops always ready and waiting by the stove in case he dropped in unannounced and wanted something to eat. His other demand was for silence, an important consideration for someone who read voraciously – for many years he had an arrangement with a local bookseller to buy every single book in *any language* which touched on the subject of electricity – and he would go to great lengths to ensure that he was not disturbed while hard at it.

Besides forbidding servants to speak to him unless he spoke first – a common enough request among rich landowners, if this book is any guide – he kept the window shutters closed for much of the day, and did much of his best work at night after taking dinner – mutton, presumably – at around 2 a.m. He once paid £20,000 to have a local road rerouted away from his estate after deciding that motorised traffic levels were becoming too high, and would insist that newborn lambs were immediately removed from any sheep grazing in the park lest their bleating disturb his thoughts. (Noisome pheasant, partridge and quail were similarly culled from the estate, although – somewhat curiously – his gamekeepers were repeatedly told to warn anyone off from harming any of the pigeons.)

Between the ages of nineteen and fifty he worked away in silence, eventually securing around twenty individual patents on his ideas. Most over this period were concerned with electrical contraptions, although he was also interested in telegraphy, chemistry, the science of aeronautics, iron manufacture and brick-making. Ahead of his twentieth birthday he succeeded in perfecting the single-needle telegraph, a device which had the advantage of requiring less power than conventional alternatives. It attracted the attention of the Bank of England, a number of railway companies and the Electric Telegraph Company which planned to establish communications overland from London to New York via Siberia, Alaska, Canada and California.

What really distinguishes Dering from the average independently wealthy boffin, however, was his hobby: tightrope walking. He was good at it too, good enough to strike up a friendship with Jean François Gravelet, aka the Great Blondin, and to work with him from time to time.

Ahead of the latter's spectacular crossing 160ft above the Niagara Falls, the two of them were observed rehearsing on a wire stretched across Hertfordshire's somewhat less spectacular River Mimram. A very minor waterway which rises north of Whitwell and flows into the Lea at Hertford, Dering's role was reasonably hazardous but utterly passive and saw him trussed up in a sack and dumped in a wheelbarrow while a blindfolded Blondin pushed him across the wire.

He never troubled to explain his interest in this strange pursuit, and it took until 1907, a mere four years before his death, for the inventor finally to explain his long absences from Lockleys and his Irish estate.

It turned out that he was married after all, and had lived for much of his life incognito and in Brighton where he had a wife and daughter. Down there he was known only as Mr Dale, and so successful was he at separating the two halves of his strangely productive life that the first his daughter knew of his immense wealth and the Lockleys estate was when she inherited the lot, lock, stock and barrel, following her eccentric parent's demise in 1911.

NORTH MYMMS PARK, nr Hatfield

A Jacobean house surrounded by 120 acres of parkland, North Mymm's chequered history has seen the manor in the ownership of a number of families, starting from the Coningsbys progressing through the Duke of Leeds and then back to another Coningsby.

One of those who expected to get it at some point was Colonel Charles de Laet Waldo Sibthorp MP (1783–1855). A fairly distant Coningsby relative, his parents had named him after one of the family's legatees – the old, unmarried and childless Charles de Laet – in the hope that eventually all their wealth and estates would come to him.

In the end they failed to do so, although his grandson eventually took possession about fifteen years after Sibthorp's death. The colonel seems not to have let any of this bother him, however, being instead much too concerned for much of his life with complaining about pretty much everything and objecting to progress in all its forms.

In Brewer's *Rogues, Villains and Eccentrics* he is described as having set 'a standard of reaction and xenophobia unequalled, perhaps, in parliamentary history.' Dickens thought him amusing, if 'slightly damaged' in the head. Even the ordinarily highly circumspect *Dictionary of National Biography* sees in him the 'embodiment of old-fashioned prejudice,' and says his long service, the best part of thirty years as Member for Lincoln, established him as 'a notorious rather than a respected figure in public life'.

His early days were fairly routine for a man of such a background, with his time at Oxford – Brasenose was the family college – being followed by a commission in the Royal Scots Greys and then a spell in the Dragoons with whom he saw action in the Peninsular War.

Thereafter, following his election to the Commons in 1826, he lost little time in objecting to the Reform Bill, any moves at all to improve the lot of Anglo-Catholics, and the repeal of the Corn Laws.

Striding around the Palace in a distinctive get-up of a stiff blue Regency coat, tall Wellington boots, and an enormous gold quizzing glass or monocle which dangled on a long chain, Sibthorp's opinions were invariably as singular and anachronistic as his appearance. Anything he took exception to was likened to the devil – whom he 'detested' – or flagged up as likely to hasten the triumph of the 'railroads and other dangerous novelties'. Railways, indeed, were a particular bugbear, Sibthorp maintaining that they did nothing for society save encouraging the working class to travel about.

Other hearty dislikes included libraries, lavatories (he was concerned that sanitary inspectors would soon be using them to see what people had had for dinner), what he called 'opera dancers', foreigners without exception, and of course everywhere abroad which he could see no point in visiting except for the purposes of going to war. Nor did he want anyone else going there if they could possibly help it, and vigorously campaigned for a new tax payable for every day a British subject spent out of the country.

Unfortunately, while the colonel's respect for tradition and the monarchy clearly enabled him to overlook Queen Victoria's somewhat less than English antecedence, there was no getting away from the fact that this Prince Albert of Saxe-Coburg and Gotha fellow she seemed set on marrying was most definitely a Hun. That was bad enough but when it was proposed to give the man an allowance, Sibthorp saw red and quickly started lobbying his parliamentary colleagues to have the proposed amount cut to as little as possible.

Queen Victoria was naturally furious, even when the Prime Minister assured her that Sibthorp was a crank and that the proposal would go no further. In this he could not have been more wrong, however, for when the matter was put to a vote the motion was carried reducing the new Prince Consort's annuity from £50,000 to just £30,000. What the Prince thought of it is not recorded, but always happy to bear a grudge, the Queen thereafter refused to visit the city of Lincoln until Sibthorp was voted out and buried six feet under.

Sibthorp himself was far from finished, however, and was soon up in arms about the proposed Great Exhibition, Prince Albert's pet project which he characterised as 'an absurdity and a wild goose-chase'. It wasn't just this foreign prince's intention of introducing 'foreign stuff of every description', or even that the capital would be overrun by foreigners 'talking all kinds of gibberish' and peddling 'foreign trash and trumpery'. That was certainly bad enough but the chief problem seemed to be that a number of trees would need to be felled to make way for the new Crystal Palace – an 'obscene and unsanitary structure', he called it – and that the event would be a magnet for criminals who were presently 'scattered over the country.'

Fortunately his persuasive powers were this time markedly less effective, and while he continued to rail against the event and warn residents around Hyde Park to lock up their silver and servant girls, the Queen went on to cut the ribbon and the Great Exhibition rapidly proved itself to be one of the triumphs of her reign.

Something seemed to go out of Sibthorp after that, but he soldiered on nevertheless and was actually speaking in the Commons in 1855 – objecting to some small matter of expenditure overseas – when he collapsed and died. The House had doubtless lost a character, but also something of a pain in the neck.

TRING PARK, Tring

On the one hand a zoologist with an international reputation, and an acknowledged expert in the collecting and taxonomy of birds and butterflies, Lionel, 2nd Lord Rothschild (1868–1937) always known as Walter, was also the sort of man who entertained dogs to dinner. He also trained a team of zebra to pull his carriage, lived with his mother for all but three years of his life, and on more than one occasion was photographed riding a giant tortoise while encouraging this unlikely beast of burden to move forward by waving a cabbage leaf a few inches ahead of its bony nose.

Educated at Cambridge before being employed (very reluctantly) in the family bank, Walter's lifelong interest in zoology was encouraged by a meeting with the German-born zoologist Albrecht Karl Ludwig Gotthilf Günther, although by this stage his interest in collecting things was already highly advanced. (By the age of just thirteen he had been corresponding with experts, and his parents had already taken the decision to employ a full-time assistant to help him catalogue his specimens.)

Upon reaching adulthood he had embraced his passion fully, beginning the long process of transforming his home at Tring Park into something of a private zoological museum and on one occasion

spending £15,000 of his father's money on a variety of different insects. So impressive was the end result that he was eventually able to give his extensive purpose-built premises and several million zoological specimens to the British Museum, although at the time such expenditure – equivalent today to nearly £7 million – had outraged his father whose sincere wish was that he would quickly get over this collecting mania and concentrate on bank business instead.

Never one to do things by halves – his collection of specimens is almost certainly the largest of its kind in the world, even though at one point had been forced to sell an incredible 295,000 stuffed birds to pay off a titled, female blackmailer. Rothschild's speciality was the painstaking, systematic classification of the various different species. The only practical way to achieve this, he knew, was to build up his own collection – among Victorians the Rothschild family as a whole were known to exhibit something of a mania for collecting – and this he duly did before bringing the formidable powers of his computer-like intellect to bear on the not inconsiderable problems of differentiating between one species of animal and another.

Working at this sort of thing for up to fourteen hours a day, Rothschild and his staff produced many millions of words of documentation to support their work and Tring's in-house journal soon extended to more than forty bound volumes. All the while his lordship and the team sat surrounded by more than 2,000 stuffed animals, including every type of zebra known to man, 2,400 stuffed birds, 300 dried reptiles, 640 other reptiles, 200 mounted heads, 300 pairs of antlers, 1,400 animal skins and skulls, 300,000 bird skins, more than 300,000 beetles, 200,000 birds' eggs and an incredible 2.25 million different insects.

Needless to say seekers after the curious would not have come away from Tring dissatisfied either, since the collection also included several extinct species including the quagga, the thylacine, a great auk, the giant sloth – the skeleton of which really is gigantic – a moa and a dodo. The collection also included a unique preserved specimen of a young zebroid, a stripy horsey-hybrid beast, which had been bred by the great man himself.

Best of all, at least for our purposes, Lord Rothschild never made even the slightest attempt to be normal. Thus on one occasion as the Member for Aylesbury – he was not a great speaker, but lobbied strongly for a national home for the Jewish people – he outraged the Commons by taking his seat wearing a white top hat. On another occasion he drove a carriage and four-in-hand down the Mall and into the courtyard of Buckingham Palace – three of the four in this case being zebra, which Queen Alexandra thought charming. And while a speech defect made him painfully shy with women he also took absolutely no care to keep his assignations with actresses and young socialites secret – except from his mother, hence the aforementioned blackmailing incident.

Finally, of course, he is almost certainly the only Member of Parliament to have a species of giraffe named after him, the five-horned Rothschild, Uganda or Baringo Giraffe, *Giraffa camelopardalis rothschildi*. Indeed, as the Israeli newspaper *Haaretz* gleefully reported long after the death of this great Zionist, 'another 153 insects, 58 birds, 17 mammals, three fish, three spiders, two reptiles, one millipede and one worm also carry his name.'

Kent

Imagine a man who used soda water to dilute the most expensive claret, who only ever travelled on a Tube train once (although for a while there were plans for him to spend the war living in an old abandoned Underground station beneath Mayfair) and who rationed himself to a mere eight or nine massive cigars a day because he recognised that they weren't that good for him. Now ask yourself, how it is that when people draw up lists of celebrated English eccentrics Sir Winston Spencer Churchill's name rarely makes the cut?

His wife Clementine hit the nail on the head when she told his doctor that Churchill 'knows nothing of the life of ordinary people', and it is not hard to imagine the fate of any modern politician who, on visiting a council estate for the first time, wondered aloud how the people living there got by without 'ever eating anything savoury, and never saying anything clever'. WSC did precisely this, however, yet somehow not only got away with it but went on to become the most popular political leader in a thousand years of British history.

In fact more than popular, Churchill is loved and revered like none other. Of course winning the war to end all wars will have helped, but that was only part of it. Somehow it didn't matter that he never, ever went on a bus, because no-one expected him to do the sorts of things we do every day. It didn't matter that he was fat, bald and had a lisp – image was clearly much less important for public figures than it is now – or that he wore pink underwear and even zip-up Oxfords beneath the frankly pretty bizarre 'siren suits' he favoured and which, one-piece and ketchup-coloured, even his own family likened to oversized rompers. He was, in short, a one-off.

Born in a ladies' loo at Blenheim Palace, briefly the heir to one of the great dukedoms, and via his American mother one-sixteenth Iroquois Indian, after the disaster of Gallipoli Churchill's response to what could have been the end of his career was to say the least unexpected.

To cheer himself up he went home, got out his Meccano – of which he had a huge collection for just such occasions – and built a scale model of the Forth Rail Bridge. Bricklaying was another unlikely hobby for such an obviously old-fashioned aristocrat – at Chartwell he built wall after wall as another kind of stress-buster – and he reportedly liked the

film *That Hamilton Woman* so much that he watched Vivien Leigh and Laurence Olivier in it at least 100 times.

Also, for a man who is commonly likened to a tough, no-nonsense British bulldog, one wonders what on earth is to be made of the fact that his favourite animals were cats, poodles and a green budgie called Toby – and several hundred butterflies, although these he chloroformed and pinned. (He kept horses too, but more for racing than riding, and regretted promising one of them a lifetime of 'agreeable female company' if he won – only to see the nag come in fourth because this exciting prospect meant he was not able to 'keep his mind on the race'.)

Finally, the great man also seems to have had a bit of a uniform fetish, and at various times was photographed wearing both Army and Royal Air Force uniforms, although by this time he was well into his mid-sixties and could by no means be considered to be on active military service. Curiously he was never snapped in Royal Navy rig, however, despite being First Lord of the Admiralty, although he made up for this by appearing alongside President Roosevelt – Churchill's sixth cousin, incidentally – wearing a reefer jacket and cap in the rather singular livery of the Royal Yacht Squadron.

His excuse for such a get up was that he had joined the club back in 1911, prompting the historian A.J.P. Taylor later to observe that the country had been 'led to victory by a sardonic old fellow who wore funny clothes and drank wine at breakfast.' That sums him up rather nicely, but hopefully without losing sight of the fact that he was a Very Great Man.

CHEVENING HOUSE, Chevening, nr Sevenoaks

The seat of the Earls Stanhope from the early eighteenth century until 1967 when it was presented to the nation, Chevening these days pays host to plenty of interesting people in its capacity as the official country residence of the Foreign Secretary although there has arguably been none to equal Lady Hester Stanhope who was born there in 1776.

An intrepid traveller at a time when it was the lot of most upper class women – and virtually all earls' daughters – to do little more than find a husband and settle down, Lady Hester was awarded a pension of £1,200 a year at the age of thirty, much of which went on paying her way around the world. The money was a grateful nation's way of thanking her for playing hostess to the unmarried Pitt the Younger (her uncle), and such was her fame that when she reached Greek waters Lord Byron is said to have dived into the sea at Athens and swum out to greet her.

With Pitt gone, her life had become boring although the main reason for her going was that she believed she was to going to be crowned Queen of the East. That this prophecy had come from an inmate of Bethlehem Royal Hospital – more commonly known as Bedlam, London's leading lunatic asylum – seemed not to bother her, perhaps because she had been looking for an excuse to escape these shores since childhood.

As a child, having given her governess the slip, she had found a small boat and attempted unsuccessfully to row to France. As an adult she was rather more successful, jumping aboard the frigate *Jason* and exploring the countries bordering the eastern Mediterranean until she was shipwrecked between Cairo and Constantinople. Losing her clothes in the disaster, she borrowed a turban and robe from a local chap, deciding never again to dress in European clothes (or for that matter as a woman) and to spend the rest of her days roaming around the east.

Surprisingly the locals took to her, admiring her spirit and courage and for some reason accepting her refusal to cover her face. If nothing else the respect accorded to her in this way confirmed Lady Hester's belief that she was destined for great things. Her belief that she would become the Messiah's bride grew still stronger when Jerusalem's Church of the Holy Sepulchre was thrown open in her honour, and again when a number of fortune-tellers and mystics appeared to echo the Bedlam prophecy.

Before long, in her purple velvet robe, gold-embroidered trousers, blood-red saddle and white-hooded cloak, Lady Hester became a familiar sight at a number of holy sites and was received by local and religious dignitaries including desert sheikhs and the Emir Mahannah el Fadel.

Arriving at Palmyra in Syria she was treated to a kind of coronation, after which she let it be known that from now on she should be addressed only as Queen Hester. She also announced that her odyssey was drawing to a close, and that she intended to establish a new 'court' of her own in a disused monastery at Mar Elias on a spur of Mount Lebanon.

Clearly a pension of £1,200 still went a long way in the Levant, and before long the ruined monastery had been rebuilt and refitted, and extended to include new stable buildings and a gazelle house. But still waiting for the call from the Messiah, Lady Hester nevertheless decided to move on, setting up a second court in another abandoned monastery at D'joun. Here, robed and enthroned, she received her visitors graciously in the hope that a chosen one would bring her a message confirming that the prophecy was about to be fulfilled.

Alas none did, and as Lady Hester slipped into old age, her fortunes slowly turned. Faithful servants were replaced by light-fingered ones, the respect of others gave way to ridicule, and her air of audacity and authority gradually became one of confusion, unwarranted self-importance and disappointment.

Eventually, alarmed by stories of profligacy and debt, the British government took steps to cut off her allowance. Letters of protest to Lord Palmerston and Queen Victoria went unanswered and by the time of her death, in 1839 aged sixty-three, Lady Hester Stanhope cut a fairly sad and lonely figure. Broke and finally broken-spirited, it was a tragic ending for someone whose folly had been to embrace the excitement and romance of the mysterious east rather than slipping into the stifling spinsterhood that would have been her lot in nineteenth-century England.

COLD HARBOUR, West Malling

The original 'Disgusted of Tunbridge Wells' – in fact he lived in West Malling – Lieutenant-Colonel Alfred Daniel Wintle MC (1897–1966) was born in Russia, schooled in France and educated in Germany but nevertheless got down on his knees every night of his life 'and thanked God for making me an Englishman'. Sadly history fails to relate whether he knew Sir Claude Champion de Crespigny (see p. 55) but it seems likely that, being cut from the same piece of fine English worsted, the two of them would have had plenty to talk about had they met over a couple of generous club measures.

A career cavalryman in the 1st Royal Dragoons and later the 11th Hussars, Wintle sincerely believed that time spent anywhere but the back of a horse was time wasted. He also carried an umbrella wherever he went and regardless of the forecast. There was, he thought, no greater symbol of an Englishman's superiority over other races, and so 'no gentleman ever leaves home without one.' This somewhat startling declaration was invariably followed by another of his favourite *bon mots*, that neither would a true gentleman ever unfurl or actually use an umbrella in public.

Like many serving officers he noted the date in his diary when the First World War ended, only then to use the very next page to demonstrate how impatient he was for another one to begin by inscribing it 'Wintle declares war on Germany'. With this in mind he set about petitioning the War Office for some affirmative action, apparently believing that organisation's sole function was to ready the nation for the next big scrap – and to see that it was not long in coming.

It was perhaps inevitable that when hostilities did finally break out Wintle would find himself entirely dissatisfied with the way authorities planned to deal with their historic enemy. Because of this he decided to have a go at them in his own special fashion instead, and after attempting to commandeer an aeroplane to get him to the front in double-quick time, Wintle quickly found himself in the Tower of London awaiting a court martial.

His plan had been to destroy the French air force before Germany could lay hands on it, but instead the charge was that he had pulled a revolver on an Air Ministry official after being denied access to the aeroplane he needed to get himself there. It is also believed he signed his own travel warrant to get to the Tower, having become so irritated at the RAF's apparent inability to get the job done properly.

His enthusiasm undimmed by this minor setback – tenacity was his middle name – Wintle took his batman with him into captivity to ensure his personal comfort, and then set about inviting many eminent and influential guests to dine with him each evening. The result of this was that when his case finally came to trial the higher echelons were sufficiently embarrassed to quietly drop it and to arrange for him to be sent abroad.

Soon imprisoned as a spy in occupied France, and recaptured after a courageous but unsuccessful escape, the monocled Wintle refused to let his standards drop and famously took his Vichy captors to task for their sloppy habits and scruffy demeanour. Deciding to go on a hunger strike until they smartened up their act, he was soon to be heard loudly and repeatedly insisting that to a man they were a shambles and as such wholly unfit to hold an officer in the King's Army.

Nearly two decades later, on ITV's *This is Your Life* programme, the head of the garrison in question admitted to an audience of literally millions that he and more than 200 of his men had eventually switched sides after this incident – 'entirely because of the Colonel's dauntless example and his tirade of abuse and challenge.' Clearly the force of Wintle's personality was something to be reckoned with – as indeed he was to demonstrate again while in hospital after falling from his horse.

During his stay there he discovered that someone from his own regiment was in an adjacent bed, a young boy-trumpeter apparently suffering from the usually fatal combination of diphtheria and mastoiditis. Standing over him, Wintle roared, 'What's all this nonsense about you dying, man? You know it's against regulations for a Royal Dragoon to die in his bed. You will stop dying at once, get up immediately and get your bloody hair cut!' Remarkably the young man, Cedric Mays, did just that, admitting later that after Wintle's outburst he was simply 'too terrified to die'.

Eventually forced to leave his beloved regiment and to accept retirement and a life in Civvy Street, Wintle settled down near West Malling in Kent while continuing his one-man battle to defend what he saw as proper English standards of behaviour.

Inevitably this sometimes brought him into trouble with the law: on one occasion, having purchased a first-class rail ticket and finding no seat free, he took the driver's place and refused to give it up until an extra carriage was found for him. He also served six months in Wormwood Scrubs for debagging a bent solicitor, whose trousers he had intended running up a flagpole. Released from prison for good behaviour, Wintle was later able to clear his name in a landmark case, one which – characteristically – he fought all the way to the House of Lords while representing himself rather than engaging the services of one of the solicitor's equally dubious colleagues.

Tricky, prickly, troublesome, highly chauvinistic and almost certainly a bit too keen on flogging, it is nevertheless hard not to miss the likes of Lt-Col A.D. Wintle – a man who, in his own words, having spent a lifetime fighting clots eventually died of one. At his funeral service at Maidstone Crematorium (he had been refused a bigger show at Canterbury Cathedral, with the band of the Royal Dragoons) he was played out by a bugle at the lips of the aforementioned Cedric Mays.

DOWN HOUSE, Downe, nr Orpington (EH)

Long-lived, academically highly distinguished, and a respected Fellow of the Royal Society who was sufficiently well connected to establish his own professorial chair at London University, the great misfortune of Sir Francis Galton (1822–1911) has been to go down in history as some kind of a proto-Nazi nutter with a penchant for silly hats and an overdeveloped interest in the overdeveloped bottoms of African women.

The racist slur is made on the basis of Galton's interest in selective breeding, a subject in which his interest was aroused by reading his cousin Charles Darwin's groundbreaking work, *On the Origin of Species*, and discussing its contents at length with the great man during frequent visits to the latter's home here in Kent. Unfortunately Galton's cogitations later attracted the attention of Heinrich Himmler among others, since when his reputation has been badly tainted by this unwelcome and unasked for association with the Third Reich.

In his lifetime, however, Galton was accorded rather more respect, being recognised as a pioneering statistician, the founding father of the science of fingerprinting – something he somehow stumbled upon while looking for a way of quantifying colour-blindness in Quakers – an early enthusiast for IQ tests, and the creator of the world's first weather map. His passionate promotion of scientific eugenics (a word Galton coined himself) was also considered perfectly respectable at the time by colleagues at the Royal Society, although these days one instinctively recoils from anything which even hints at improving humankind by promoting a more organised approach to reproduction.

Aside from the triumphs, however, there is no doubt that some of his enquiries tended at times to lead Sir Francis down some very strange roads indeed. It is also all too easy to see that his enthusiasm for collecting and collating accurate data could definitely leave Sir Francis Galton open to the charge of being more than a little barmy.

Who else, after all, would bother to invent a pocket-sized device in order to count the number of pretty women he encountered during the course of his working day? To fit his house with an aircraft-style device designed to indicate and record when and how often the loo was used? To swear by the use of gunpowder as an emetic? Or indeed to carry a brick around with him so as to have something handy to stand on whenever he needed to see over the heads of other, slightly taller people?

He was an oddball, no question, although of course the pretty girl-counter, which today would have him arrested for stalking, eventually more than paid its way once its creator had got it home and started to manipulate the data. Using it to draw up what he called a *Beauty Map of Britain* – this of course took many months of research out in the field – Galton the expert statistician soon concluded that London had the highest proportion of pretty girls, and Aberdeen the lowest (although strangely the map was to prove a bestseller north of the border when copies finally went on sale.)

Unfortunately the same counter was later used to measure the incidence of blue eyes and blonde hair in passers-by, which was part of Galton's scheme for advancing what he called racial perfection. It was this research which long after his death led Himmler to describe him as a 'great Englishman', and which in turn still means that few observers these days are willing to risk dismissing the casually racist Sir Francis Galton as just another harmless eccentric.

A keen and energetic traveller who would routinely break raw eggs into his boots to soften the leather, Galton also attempted to put a figure on different national levels of dishonesty and eventually concluded (without much surprise) that the English were the most honest folk in Europe, and the Greeks the least. As noted above he also devised a way of measuring Hottentot rear-ends, a curious field of study to say the least, eventually deciding to use a sextant for his fieldwork after recognising that collecting the same data using a tape measure might be to invite hostility and even violence from his subjects.

It is true that a century on some of his ideas require very little explanation: to keep your clothes dry in a storm, for example, his advice was to take them off and sit on them. But others require a bit more understanding, such as his complex mathematical equations for calculating the resemblance between two people, or for that matter the workings of the miniature pressure sensors which he had fitted to his dining room chairs in order (he said) to gauge how much his dinner guests liked or disliked each other.

Apparently, having noticed that guests who found each other engaging tended to lean towards each other when they talked (and that the reverse was true of those who did not) Galton had wanted to find a way of putting a value on each relationship. Whereas most of us would probably be content to observe how freely or not the conversation flowed between one friend and another over dinner, and to take an approximate measure from this, Galton decided to use his pressure sensors as a way of measuring the inclination of each chair which he then planned to use to gauge the level of engagement between one guest and the next.

Unsurprisingly perhaps for someone who claimed to have sprained his brain reading Mathematics at Cambridge, Sir Francis was also obsessive about cranial health, especially his own. This was something he sought to optimise with yet another invention, a perfect example of Heath-Robinson headgear which had it gone on sale would doubtless have been called something like Galton's Universal Patent Ventilating Hat.

Based on his belief in something unspecified but perhaps akin to medieval 'humors', the hat in question was fitted with a valve which was opened and closed using a rubber bulb which would hang down conspicuously over the wearer's shoulder. Using this, the wearer could prevent his head overheating – thereby, as Sir Francis politely informed his fellow dinner guests, avoiding the possibility of embarrassing his hostess 'by falling into a fit upon the floor'.

While he received many great honours during his lifetime, including a knighthood, Sir Francis was aware that he had never really connected with the common man. In his last year of life he worked hard on a novel which he hoped would propagate some of this theories in much the same way that *Origins* had done for Darwin. He called it *Kantsaywhere*, describing a utopia defined by a eugenic religion and in which the aim of life was to breed smarter, fitter citizens. He failed to find a publisher, however, and eventually entrusted it to a favourite niece in the hope that she would see it through the presses after he was gone. Unfortunately she seems to have incinerated most of the manuscript after deciding that her uncle's sex scenes were offensive, and that was that for *Kantsaywhere*.

HOWLETTS, nr Canterbury

Gambler, zookeeper, self-confessed misanthrope and a would-be right-wing revolutionary, more than a decade after his passing there is still something of the Regency about John Victor Aspinall (1926–2000) and his commitment to a style of life which had disappeared long before he arrived in London from India and began to make his mark.

Today he is most commonly associated with gorillas and big cats, having established families of both at Port Lympne and Howletts, the private zoos he established at his two country houses in Kent. The money to do this came from gambling rather than any inheritance, the man he assumed was his father having been an Army surgeon and his actual one a brother officer with whom his middle-class mother was having an affair.

The gambling started early, and at Jesus College, Oxford, the rakish Aspinall skipped his finals to be at Ascot where he won a tidy sum. Before long he was running illegal games in London, moving from one prestigious address to another to stay ahead of the authorities. When the law changed to allow private clubs to operate, he opened the Clermont in Berkeley Square which quickly became the headquarters of a new 'Mayfair Set'. Attracting five dukes, a similar number of marquesses and another two dozen peers, members included some 600 high-rollers in all, including Aspinall's friends Sir James Goldsmith and the ill-fated 7th Earl of Lucan (*q.v.*).

When the latter disappeared, apparently after bludgeoning his children's nanny to death having mistaken her for his estranged wife, Aspinall lost no time in showing where his loyalties lay. Showing scant sympathy for the nanny, and none at all for the wife, he was happy to tell the press that 'Lucky' Lucan had done the right thing. 'A very brave thing', he called it, going out like a gentleman by deliberately scuttling his speedboat off Newhaven and 'down he went'.

It wasn't that the tall, rangy club proprietor liked Lucan particularly, or simply that his personal code meant he would always stick by his friends. Mostly he felt only contempt for humanity – certainly that section of it which wrote for and read the tabloids – and he subsequently admitted that of his thirty best friends at least half were animals. Here he was happy to put his money where his mouth was, and spent literally tens of millions on the establishment and upkeep of his two zoos.

His commitment to the two zoos was total – reportedly barely a quarter of the annual running costs were recovered in ticket sales – but so was his belief in his animals. When asked whether his own children were safe playing with them, he memorably replied in his booming, patrician voice that he would 'rather leave them with the gorillas than with a social worker'; similarly when he fell ill with cancer in his seventies, he seriously considered allowing one of his tigers to finish him off. (Aspinall was also more than once quoted as saying he would be entirely happy to sacrifice his own children if this would help save another species from becoming extinct.)

In fact with strong leanings towards this extreme sort of Darwinism, Aspinall had quite lot to say about the application of natural or jungle law to humanity. For example, with overcrowding becoming such a huge problem, he could see nothing whatever wrong with allowing malaria to kill off two billion of the worst undesirables. He was equally dismissive of the idea of sexual equality, pointing to his own wife whom he described as 'the perfect example of the primate female, ready to serve the dominant male and make his life agreeable.' (He was twice divorced.)

Today, unsurprisingly, opinion about him is as divided as ever it was, although it is hard to think that he would mind either way what others thought of him. On the one hand his unorthodox approach to animal breeding repeatedly produced far better results than many larger, better-funded establishments could lay claim to. It is also possible to argue (as Aspinall himself did) that by admitting only toffs and plutocrats to the Clermont and his other clubs he did more than anyone since Karl Marx to bring about the redistribution of wealth and the ruination of the rich.

The other side is far less appealing, however. Always a controversial and contradictory character, he remained convinced, for example, that Hitler was largely correct about eugenics – and thought it entirely sensible for people to feel that they were members of a particular tribe and to believe in the idea that they were superior to others. Instinct and prejudice, he felt, were much more reliable guides to behaviour than mere reason, and earthquakes and plagues were to be welcomed as perfectly natural solutions to problems such as starvation, dependency and global over-population.

Finally one is left with a distinctly uneasy feeling that, while it was Aspinall himself who most loved promoting the idea of closer bonding with dangerous wild animals (he was frequently photographed wrestling with tigers and gorillas), it was his zoo workers who sometimes paid the price. No fewer than five of them were crushed or mauled to death during Aspinall's own lifetime, and at least two visitors were badly injured. Faced with what he saw as council meddling, Aspinall's response was characteristically abrupt and typically aloof: immediately threatening to close both zoos down if any attempt was made to prevent his keepers entering his enclosures with his animals, he observed that 'one tiger in 12 has this aberrant streak. With humans, it is one in three.'

KNOLE HOUSE, nr Sevenoaks (NT)

It's not hard to guess how the chippy, snobbish and increasingly misanthropic Vita Sackville-West would have reacted to the thought of her precious Sissinghurst Castle being thrown open to the general public, but her mother is a rather more difficult character to assess.

Certainly her combination of Latin passion and Anglo-Saxon reserve would have marked her out from the crowd, Victoria-Josefa Dolores Catalina, Lady Sackville (1862–1936) being the result of an illicit affair between a Spanish dancer called Pepita and an English diplomat. But more than this it was her relationship to money which stands out today, Victoria-Josefa demonstrating on the one hand a complete lack of understanding about its true value – she once left a £10,000 cheque made out to cash in the back of a cab – and on the other such incredible meanness as to spend an entire afternoon cutting up old postage stamps to save a few pennies by sticking the unfranked portions back together again and reusing them the following day.

Her stinginess seemed to know no bounds. The franked portions of stamps, the bits she couldn't reuse, would eventually be stuck up in place of wallpaper, and her desk drawers and bathrooms were always

stuffed with headed paper stolen from hotels and loo rolls lifted from the ladies' room at Harrods. It goes without saying that she wasn't one to waste money on coal or firewood either and the wind fairly whipped through Knole House with Lady Sackville insisting all doors and windows were pinned open (even in the winter) while in place of a scarf she tied together an old pair of socks reputed to have once belonged to the architect Sir Edwin Lutyens.

Curiously for one with such a celebrated gardener as a daughter, Lady Sackville very much preferred porcelain and metal flowers to real ones, and once decorated her garden with coloured velvet and sequinned paper in place of anything more conventional. Fortunately the staff mostly took such peccadilloes for granted, although more than once they quit en masse when an old nanny who had been in service with the family for decades was fired after being accused of stealing and consuming several dozen quail which had gone missing.

Like many a miser Lady Sackville worried constantly about money, and her perceived lack of it. During the First World War this led her to write to Lord Kitchener asking that her husband not be sent anywhere dangerous. This was not because she loved him, which she may have done, but because she was concerned that the family would never be able to pay the death duties if he succumbed to something awful while serving in the trenches.

She wasn't above begging for money either, and while on occasion this was for others less fortunate than herself, it is generally now accepted that – as her Ladyship was never quite able to distinguish between charity and racketeering – most of the money sent to her at Knole House in all likelihood probably stayed there.

This view is firmly reinforced by the fact that none of the Charity Commissioners had even heard of Lady Sackville's Homeless Sleeping on Brighton Beach charity – sole officer and trustee: Lady Sackville – nor one imagines of the Roof of Friendship Fund which she set up a few years later in 1928. That she became so cross when one of those she approached gave her a tile instead of actual cash would also suggest that the roof in question was the leaky one at Knole, rather than some larger, more spiritual organisation dedicated to bringing succour to the homeless.

It's also worth mentioning that she could show considerable ingenuity too – or perhaps that should just be chutzpah – especially when it came to relieving others of their small change. For example, in an attempt to clear the National Debt (so she said) Lady Sackville set up what she called the Million Penny Fund. To help it along she intended to obtain a penny-for-every-year from anyone whose birthday was mentioned in the newspaper, something she set out to achieve by writing to the relevant people and asking them to return to her a penny for every year they had been alive.

She also insisted they send her three stamped addressed envelopes with the money: one to refund to her the cost of the original begging letter, another to enable her to write back to say thank you for the donation, and of course a third 'for a fresh victim'.

At the very least she was thus being paid twice for the one letter, and while it is still not known how much the Million Penny Fund raised in the end – in today's money, by the way, that mighty-sounding sum is just a little over £4,166 – readers will know that the National Debt is still very much with us, and has never been higher than it is today.

MOUNT MORRIS, Monks Horton

Only very briefly a Member of Parliament, Matthew Robinson (1712–1800) was reportedly so shocked by the corruption endemic in party politics that he resigned almost as soon as he was elected. On succeeding his father as Lord Rokeby he then decided to withdraw to Kent where he set about installing his own brand of democracy and natural justice on the family's 800-acre estate.

His first move was a decision never to raise the tenants' rents, his second an insistence that the fields around Mount Morris should be farmed entirely according to his own radical views on agriculture and animal husbandry. This meant no fences and no closed gates, and no trees were to be felled anywhere or anything planted or cultivated but that which grew naturally. Before long the gardens were returned to nature – or ruin, depending on your perspective – while flocks of sheep and herds of cattle were allowed to roam and graze wherever they wanted, on the sensible grounds that they probably knew better than their keepers what they liked to eat.

Rokeby's approach to personal grooming was equally odd, allowing his beard to run down to his knees, and his moustaches – of which there were definitely two – to grow so long that he could flip them over his ears while his beard was divided between his armpits. He also preferred to walk everywhere, being a huge fan of fresh air and frequent exercise, and was always happy for his servants to come along for company and to do so while travelling in his carriage.

His other great health tip concerned the use of water, which he recommended to everyone for both internal and external applications.

To deal with the former he set up drinking fountains all over his estate, providing small monetary rewards for any tenants or staff he observed drinking from them. As for the latter he spent many hours of each day immersed in the stuff, spending hours swimming in the sea at Hythe and later going so far as to have a special saltwater pool house built on the estate.

The pool itself was relatively small, the building housing it quaintly thatched, and Rokeby would sit in it up to his neck for much of the day. Thus arranged he would take meals, while entertaining visitors or researching and writing a series of pamphlets in which he laid out his various theories and political philosophies. His meals, incidentally, always included beef tea, occasionally venison, and locally grown alternatives to conventional imports – such as honey instead of cane sugar, and burnt peas in place of coffee.

Convinced all doctors were charlatans – his cure for every ailment seemed to be more beef tea while sitting with the windows open and no fire lit – Rokeby also had the lowest possible opinion of the Bank of England and its officials. Such an institution, he insisted, was sure to fail in the end – and indeed he was so sure of this that he not only made a substantial £10 bet on it with a Canterbury bigwig but took steps to ensure that his heirs would continue the bet should he die before the bank. This he did in 1800, aged eighty-seven, with the wager, presumably, still running.

SISSINGHURST, nr Cranbrook (NT)

Never fully coming to terms with her loss of Knole House – she was the 3rd Lord Sackville's only child but the laws of primogeniture meant both estate and barony went to a more distant male heir – Vita Sackville-West described the subsequent gift of the house to the National Trust as 'a betrayal of all the tradition of my ancestors and the house I loved'.

Sissinghurst Castle was supposed to make up for the loss, although as a so-called calendar house – covering at least half a dozen acres, Knole is said to have 365 rooms, 52 staircases, 12 entrances and 7 courtyards – it would have taken something pretty special to match her ancestral family home. Sissinghurst came nowhere close. It may have been much, much older (Edward I stayed the night there in 1305) but it was far less grand, little more than a cluster of ruinous farm buildings and an admittedly rather lovely sixteenth-century gatehouse at the time she and her husband the writer Harold Nicolson put in an offer for it in 1930.

Famously bisexual and equally, relentlessly, exhaustingly unfaithful to their marriage vows, the two of them made, to say the least, a decidedly odd couple. Embarrassingly obsessed with their own status, both relative to each other and collectively when it came to anyone else, their snobbishness reached such a peak that they even had a private language to describe those they looked down on. A Sackville family word 'bedint' was widely used to denote any despised middle-class characteristics or attitudes, while 'bungaloid masses' was a favoured term for the plebs.

For a while the pair had lived quite happily at Long Barn near Sevenoaks, but as new developments crept ever nearer the threatened proximity of the proletariat (whom Sackville-West 'hated'), it was enough to persuade both of them that it was time to move on.

Sissinghurst at this time seemed to offer the perfect refuge as well as boasting a useful if rather distant Sackville-West connection which would have appealed to their absurd and increasingly stifling sense of dynasty. Together the two set out to rescue the buildings and the grounds, although here too they continued their childish class war by instructing the three gardeners to avoid particular species, including azaleas – because these were 'Ascot, Sunningdale sort of plants' – and rhododendrons which the new owners likened to 'fat stockbrokers, whom we do not want to have to dinner.'

What Sackville-West thought about foreigners can perhaps be gauged from her prevailing upon Nicolson to abandon a successful career as a diplomat (because she refused to consider becoming a mere embassy wife). When he did quit the service for politics she was just as unsupportive, declining point-blank an invitation to join him in Leicester where he was campaigning for a seat, and idiotically declaring 'I hate democracy. I hate *la populace*.'

The modern world she felt to be entirely 'loathsome' – a feeling which must surely have been reciprocated – and as a perfect egocentric she struggled in vain to view the Second World War as anything but an attack on her personally. The massed deaths and ruination of the Blitz she met with little complaint, but when a bomb fell on Knole she was quick to condemn 'those filthy Germans' and to call for the Air Force to 'level every town in Germany to the ground'.

When the Beveridge Report was published in 1942, her response to the idea of a new welfare state was equally predictable. After learning of this pioneering and sincere attempt to solve the very real social problems of squalor, ignorance, want and idleness, she railed against 'the proletariat being encouraged to breed like rabbits, because each new rabbit means eight shillings a week – as though there weren't enough of them already.' Perhaps surprisingly, she stopped short of actually wanting to destroy them, but when pressed admitted that she wished education had never been introduced, and that for her it would be enough to known the masses were 'as well-fed and as well-housed as cows', but no more than that.

Unfortunately Nicolson was little better and after losing at Leicester (and failing to obtain a much desired peerage from Clement Attlee) he switched to the Labour Party solely in the belief that he might get a peerage there instead. Happily he didn't, nor a seat at Croydon in the next election – after admitting that he hated 'canvassing these dumb idiots' and sincerely believed the lower classes to be 'congenitally ignorant'.

Tragically (or perhaps that should be hilariously) a large part of his motivation for wanting a title was because he had 'always hated the name Nicolson as being a common plebian name'. Musing on this he clearly spent quite a lot of his time trying to decide what title to take when one was offered – much in the manner of a foolish young girl practicing a new signature ahead of her wedding, although in Nicolson's case this was before a suitor had even been identified.

Needless to say Sackville-West liked the idea of his getting a peerage too: not 'for snobbish reasons,' she said (with a spectacular lack of conviction) but because 'I would like the boys to be Hon.' But in the end they had to make do with a mere knighthood, a title both of them felt to be irredeemably third-rate, vulgar and (horror or horrors) decidedly middle-class. Because of this, and to the end of her life, Vita Sackville-West refused to be known as 'Lady Nicolson'.

Even now, more than fifty years later and with both monsters dead and buried, the spectacle is to say the least strange of Sissinghurst Castle Gardens thronging with paying visitors. So too the veritable cult of adoration which has grown up around 'Vita and Harold', for whatever the public think of them we know very well what they would have thought of the public and their being here. Even Sir Harold, after all, had been expressly forbidden from entering the gatehouse, his prickly wife barring the entire world from her private kingdom and admitting only her pet dog.

Ironically, because of this, one of the chief pleasures of seeing coach loads queueing up to visit Sissinghurst these days is to imagine the high-pitched whine of Sir Harold and Lady Nicolson spinning in their graves. That and the almost audible gnashing of their teeth at the sight of the 'bungaloid masses' crawling all over their precious and really rather horrible little world.

BIRCHIN BOWER, Oldham

Now vanished beneath the sprawl of suburban Oldham, Birchin Bower was once home to Hannah Beswick (1680–1758) who lived mostly in fear of dying and in particular of being buried alive.

Then as now the fear was not an uncommon one, but in Hannah Beswick's case it was given a little added piquancy when her own brother apparently awoke from the dead just as the final nails were being driven in to his coffin. A variety of solutions were patented at the time to prevent the worst from happening, including ventilated coffins and even coffins fitted with bells which would sound should some poor unfortunate wake up and find herself six feet under.

Neither was sufficiently reassuring for Miss Beswick, however, and clearly a very wealthy woman she decided to leave her doctor a sum in her will on condition that he would visit her regularly after her death to see that everything was in order. In return for £100 the eminent Dr Charles White FRS was to examine the body of the 78-year-old, satisfy himself that she was not about to wake up, and determine the likelihood that she could ever be revived.

A professional to his fingertips, the founder of Manchester's Royal Infirmary was happy to earn what at the time was quite a handsome fee, and after assuring himself and witnesses that Miss Beswick was indeed dead White had her embalmed with tar and bandages before installing her in a glass-fronted grandfather clock. He kept this at the top of the stairs in his own house at King Street, Manchester, hidden from view behind a heavy velvet curtain (to avoid shocking unsuspecting visitors) and once a year would inspect Miss Beswick to make sure that she was still definitely dead.

He kept this up for the next fifty-seven years, walking up stairs, drawing back the curtain and in front of witnesses examining the remains of Hannah Beswick – who was by now more than 130 years old – to make sure that everything was still in order. Eventually news of the 'Manchester Mummy' spread, and far from scaring visitors the desiccated corpse of Hannah Beswick became something of an attraction for visitors to the area.

Nor does the story quite end there. Because her will had further required the body to be kept above ground for a full 100 years, the grisly relic had to be removed from the doctor's house when he himself

died in 1813. From King Street it was taken first to the local Lying-in Hospital, and then to the Manchester Museum of Natural History when the hospital closed. According to contemporary reports, it again began to draw crowds, becoming 'an object of much popular interest' among visitors to the museum.

It remained at the museum until 1868, at which point the terms of Hannah Beswick's will had been more than fully met. Thereafter, finally and officially declared dead at the age of 188, her body was removed for the fourth and one imagines final time, to an unmarked plot in Manchester's General Cemetery. After a proper Christian burial the Manchester Mummy was committed to the ground at last, since when there have been occasional sightings of her ghost – at the site of the Ferranti electronics factory which replaced the old house at Birchin Bower – but still nothing to suggest she is about to wake up.

Lincolnshire

GUNBY HALL, nr Spilsby (NT)

One of the first country houses to be taken on by the National Trust, eighteenth-century Gunby Hall was formerly home to Field Marshal Sir Archibald Armar Montgomery-Massingberd GCB GCVO KCMG who was reportedly very much a Victorian figure in appearance, character and demeanour although he lived on until the late 1940s.

An impressive Chief of the Imperial General Staff, and with a reputation for having fought a good war against both the Boers and Kaiser Bill, Sir Archibald thus found himself well-placed and exceptionally well-connected when it came to defending his ancestral home against the Royal Air Force which sought to build an airfield on his estate. A great patriot, and obviously not inclined to be friendly towards Germany once hostilities resumed in 1939, he fully appreciated the need for another runway, but was aghast to discover that it was to be driven through his house and grounds.

That the RAF also planned to fell 800 of his trees, mostly gloriously mature specimens planted a century earlier by Peregrine Langton Massingberd, also got Sir Archibald's goat. With what was subsequently described as 'bulldog pertinacity and fighting spirit' the old man decided to do something about it, drafting a long, well-argued letter to Chief of the Air Staff, Air Chief Marshal Portal, but receiving in reply little more than a thin statement of regret.

Undeterred, his next move was to write to the National Trust, only to be told that the organisation, which in those days had just a handful of employees, was only able to lobby on behalf of country houses it actually owned. His response was to call them in anyway, hoping against hope that their representative James Lees-Milne would find something worth saving rather than just echoing the opinion of an earlier visitor who (after renting Gunby for some shooting) found it a 'most melancholy place', which reeked of 'suicide in every room'.

Montgomery-Massingberd was in luck, Lees-Milne later writing that he 'fell for the place and its inhabitants at once.' Despite their apparent isolation out there in the wastes of Lincolnshire it seemed the childless couple were well connected (by both blood and personal inclination) to a wide circle of intellectuals and artists, and at Gunby they had managed to create almost a *salon* or at least a lively retreat for the metropolitan intelligentsia.

In his day Sir Archibald had evidently been quite a shrewd cove too, famously warning Churchill as long ago as 1918 to keep an eye on France's duplicitous Marshal Pétain, and as the threat from Hitler loomed large, he dryly observed that Prime Minister Chamberlain was not only completely ignorant of military matters but dangerously disinterested in making good that shortfall.

Gunby, in short, was probably therefore in the best possible hands at a time when its very existence was threatened. A lack of money and an heir might have spelled trouble ahead, and an insistence on dressing for dinner (even with a war on) might suggest the couple were jut comical old dinosaurs. But Montgomery-Massingberd, far from being a simple soldier, was nevertheless sufficiently wily to get the National Trust on side (by promising them the house if they could save it), and worldly enough to get another letter off to the King's private secretary, Sir Alec Hardinge.

The King, he soon learned, was 'more than sympathetic', and before long the National Trust's man – despite his earlier objections – was busy petitioning the Air Ministry in a bid to get the flyboys to see sense. With the pressure continuing to mount the RAF eventually saw no alternative but to cave in, the Secretary of State for Air writing personally to the King to assure him that the runway would now be angled away from Gunby Hall, and that only a very few trees would have to be 'topped'.

Montgomery-Massingberd, it seemed, had saved his house and soon a tall, illuminated beacon appeared on the Gunby tennis court to warn off heavy bombers coming in to land. True to his word negotiations were completed towards the end of the war, and Gunby Hall passed safely into the hands of the National Trust albeit without the organisation agreeing to the donors' initial wish that whoever got to live in it after they were gone should not be foreign or a Roman Catholic.

HARLAXTON MANOR, Harlaxton, nr Grantham

An immense ice-frosted wedding cake of a country house, nineteenth-century Harlaxton Manor – now the British campus of the University of Evansville, and full of Americans – is perhaps the nearest thing this country has to the fantastical fairytale castles of mad King Ludwig of Bavaria.

Designed in part by the young but already highly regarded Anthony Salvin, Harlaxton's High Victorian fantasy was really the creation of Mr Gregory Gregory, a bachelor who – while only modestly wealthy – took it into his head to try to outdo his neighbour the Duke of Rutland's Belvoir Castle, which he could see in the distance.

Initially he tried to do this with something Elizabethan, but soon fired Salvin and brought in the Scottish architect William Burn who moved the project towards the Jacobean. With no family attachments, and few friends to distract him, Gregory rapidly became too involved with the project for his own good, and quite at variance with his architects' previous works the house began to sprout some wildly theatrical features of a sort more in keeping with German Baroque than mid-Victorian England.

With a silhouette quite unlike any other English country house the roofline was soon festooned with scrolls and turrets, cupolas, domes and pretty parapets – every bit a case of castles in the air. Everywhere one looked there were lounging lions of bronze and marble, with lively putti reaching out for great dripping bunches of grapes, and before it all great stone piers, huge curved screen walls and porters' lodges punctuating the view from the arrow-straight, one-mile drive.

Even now the scale looks enormous – one architectural critic called it 'super-Baroque, monstrous yet imaginative' – and knowledgeable visitors can easily pass an hour standing in front of Harlaxton trying to identify the various stylistic borrowings from other, more celebrated masterpieces such as Burghley House, Rushton Hall and London's vanished Northumberland House.

If anything the inside is even more flamboyant, with tiers of cedar-wood balconies rising up through the main stair, the walls hung with more putti, enormous scallop shells and rich stucco decorations, and everything draped in great tent-like folds of plaster and oversized cast tassels. High above the scrolls and panelling and rusticated arches, a vast *trompe-l'oeil* painted sky of blue and clouds looks down on this unique theatrical set piece, Father Time enjoying the top-most vantage point with a small but detailed medallion of Gregory Gregory nearby.

Frustratingly little is known about the man himself, however, although his restless imagination and cultivated interests in gardening, books, art and sculpture would seem to mark him out from the usual new-money parvenu, the sort of man who moves to the country – in Gregory's case from Nottingham – and immediately seeks to outshine his obviously much grander and longer-established neighbours.

Sadly, but in the way of these things, he did not live long enough to enjoy what he had created. He died in 1854 before the house was completed and never managed to find a companion to live in his lavish new family wing. Instead the house was left to distant relations, and for the next eighty years it languished at the hands of a succession of widowers and ancient bachelors who lacked the wherewithal either to appreciate or to maintain Lincolnshire's whitest white elephant.

In 1937 it finally found a saviour in Mrs Violet Van der Elst, the daughter of a Surrey washerwoman who had made a fortune inventing Shavex, the world's first brushless shaving soap. Keen to leave Surrey, and looking for somewhere to hold séances and house an estimated 3,000 books on spiritualism, she was not an obvious countrywoman but answered an advertisement in *Country Life* looking for someone to save 'the labour of an age in piled stones'. Buying the empty near-ruin cost her £78,000, the restoration reportedly more than twice as much again, although when she sold it a decade later it made a paltry £60,000.

The buyer this time was the Society of Jesuits, but with insufficient novices coming in to fill such a large place they didn't stay long either, hence the switch to secular students from the USA. It is to be hoped they appreciate the mysterious Gregory Gregory's extraordinary achievement, and Harlaxton's wonderful flourishes and gloriously unapologetic vulgarity – but whether or not they do at least the great house itself is now in safe hands.

Middlesex

They say everyone loves a lord, although in the case of John James Hamilton, 1st Marquess of Abercorn (1756–1818) the likelihood is that no one loved the lord quite as much as he loved himself.

Very much one to stand on ceremony – and quite unwilling to forgive anyone who neglected to do so – this was the man who, even back in the days when he was plain Mr Hamilton, had insisted on being addressed as D'Hamilton Comte Heréditaire d'Abercorn well ahead of inheriting any such title. Similarly, when he did inherit an earldom, he successfully petitioned a busy Prime Minister to elevate his wife-to-be to the rank of an earl's daughter – which she wasn't – just to satisfy himself that he wouldn't be seen to be marrying beneath himself. (His second wife of three, when she left him he insisted she elope in his carriage, complete with his coat of arms on the doors. More than anything he was concerned that 'it ought never to be said that Lady Abercorn left her husband's roof in a hack chaise'.)

Transport arrangements clearly played an important role in Abercorn's daily life, and Sir Walter Scott was one of several acquaintances who used gleefully to tell the story of how one day he had encountered a retinue of no fewer than five carriages, numberless outriders in full livery and at its head a man on horseback bearing the blue ribbon of a Knight of the Garter. This, it seemed, was considered normal for when Hamilton went out for a little afternoon's constitutional.

Back home things were equally formal too, the housemaids being required to wear white kid gloves before touching his lordship's bed linen, and the other servants expected to rinse their hands in rosewater before Lord Abercorn would accept anything which they had touched. But perhaps the strangest thing about Abercorn was that, while he was a keen and generous host, and entirely happy for his guests to enjoy every luxury while staying at the Priory, he would at other times exhibit a reclusiveness verging on the severest sort of misanthropy.

Guests at the Priory included the great and the good, five successive prime ministers being invited to sign the visitor's book together with poets, artists and actors, and Sir Walter Scott who wrote several drafts of *Marmion* in a summerhouse on an island in the lake here. Whoever came the same rules applied, however, in particular that no guest was to speak to Hamilton directly except at mealtimes. Even then he might choose not to respond, and on at least one occasion – having invited an up-and-coming novelist to stay – the Marquess took one look at this guest from behind a curtain, and presumably deciding he did not like what he saw then slipped out through a side door and was not seen again until she had left and gone home.

TRENT PARK, nr Enfield

A stately home that now forms part of Middlesex University, Trent Park was built on a former Royal hunting ground and in the 1830s was given by the banker David Bevan to his son Robert Cooper Lee Bevan as a wedding present.

Bevan's daughter was Nesta Webster (1876–1960), an early feminist and sometime member of the British Union of Fascists whose reputation these days depends on her growing obsession with a secret society – the Illuminati – who she said were plotting to install a new world order behind a smokescreen provided by Jews, Jesuits and Freemasons.

Today such ideas are familiar if not exactly commonplace, but in large part this is itself due to Nesta Webster and her role as something of the godmother of European conspiracy theorists. It was her belief that these Illuminati (the name means 'enlightened') were implicated in – which is to say responsible for – such upheavals as the French, 1848 and Russian revolutions, and the First World War.

Her starting point for this was Paris in 1789, and a growing conviction that the Revolution was neither desired nor organised by the people of France but rather engineered from behind the scenes by a dangerous cabal, an occult power, with its origins in Bavaria. The mastermind she said was one Adam Weishaupt (1748–1830), a Jesuit lawyer turned Freemason whom Webster quickly identified as an all-purpose evil genius dedicated to the destruction of institutions of education, religion, politics and law. In the ensuing chaos and confusion, she insisted, Weishaupt and his secret society hoped to take control.

It's tempting to wonder how such a genius ever made the mistake of revealing his hand, but Webster had an answer for this too, suggesting that a secret courier for his organisation had been struck by lightning and killed. While he and his horse were completely incinerated, the documents he was carrying miraculously survived – and fell into the hands of the authorities.

Put like that (put however you like, actually) it sounds improbable but Webster was a powerful and persuasive writer, and theories of this sort seem to always find followers willing to overlook anything which fails to sound quite right. As a result publications such as *The French Terror and Russian Bolshevism*, *World Revolution: The Plot Against Civilization* and *Secret Societies and Subversive Movements* found a ready readership and Webster racked up some quite respectable sales.

It is a truism that once you see a conspiracy you begin to spot them everywhere, and rather than getting bogged down in the mechanics of how an eighteenth-century organisation in a small part of Germany might have fomented revolution in Russia, or for that matter launched the greatest war in history, Webster soon moved on. Persuading herself and her readers that the malign influence of 'grand orient Masonry, theosophy, pan-Germanism, international finance and social revolution' – the Adversary, she called it, with a capital A – had in fact been active since the very earliest times, she traced its origins to long before the appearance of the Illuminati.

Bizarrely some of her theories even garnered a measure of support from within the Establishment, the Foreign Office (perhaps losing its nerve at what was going on) officially blaming what it called 'international Jews' for the ills befalling the Romanovs, and the Brigade of Guards actually inviting her to lecture officers about the forces behind world revolution. Winston Churchill was similarly thrilling readers of a popular Sunday newspaper by appearing to agree with Webster's most lurid reports of a Jewish-Bolshevik conspiracy, but was presumably far less keen to endorse the message of a later pamphlet, *The Need for Fascism in Britain*.

In Hitler she thought she had found a useful ally – like Webster he found a use for the palpable fake that was the anti-Semitic *Protocols of the Learned Elders of Zion* – only to lose heart, like so many fellow travellers, when the Führer signed a pact with Stalin in 1939. Thereafter the stuffing went out of her somewhat, and for the remaining years of her life she became increasingly despondent about defeating the Illuminati. At the same time her once-sweeping conspiracies involving world domination gradually collapsed into a rather clichéd paranoia to which she responded by never opening her front door unless she had a gun to hand.

Eventually interest in Webster and her theories declined to the point where she was no longer able to get published. For more than a decade her autobiography did the rounds but found no takers, and was then picked up by a small right-wing press only for the manuscript to vanish for good before anyone had got round the making a copy. For the dwindling band of Webster fans the loss must have been regarded as catastrophic – but then again the mysterious disappearance of the manuscript could also be taken as yet more evidence of the all-powerful Illuminati swooping in under cover of darkness to discredit and destroy the work of those who sought to act against them.

Norfolk

Madame – as she liked to be called, with a definite French inflection – was as English as they come, being the daughter of a Baring and a niece to milords Cromer and Revelstoke. Helena, Comtesse De Noailles (1824–1908) nevertheless affected a certain Frenchness (after being briefly married to a count) together with a strange dietary and health regime which, unfortunately, she inflicted on a Spanish girl whom she had purchased and adopted when the poor child was just nine years old.

Maria Pasqua, for such was her name, was apparently bought for two bags of gold (or a vineyard, depending on who is telling the story) and was then sent to an English convent boarding school. With her went a list of requirements which was long enough to make the average modern molly-coddling parent look like they really couldn't care less what happened to their children once they'd packed them off to school.

To begin with the nuns were required to drain the school pond, for Madame had a dread of flying insects. (At home she kept a string of onions hanging by her bedroom door, presumably as some kind of odoriferous bug deterrent.) Maria herself was also forbidden to do any work after 6 p.m., to receive any inoculations against any kind of illness, and in the event of her succumbing to bronchitis the staff had orders to feed her nothing but fresh herring roe.

The school was also to provide a cow especially for Maria, in order that she, like her *maman*, would have ready access to clean, fresh milk. The same cow was also to supply fresh, health-giving methane which Madame was in the habit of obtaining by tying up her own flatulent beasts beneath the bedroom window. (Very keen on the health-giving properties of milk, mutton and methane, Madame was, and indeed had she been active a century later it is tempting to think she might have been a natural for a string of dietary bestsellers based on the 'M-Plan Diet' . . .)

Naturally Maria wasn't to wear the standard school uniform either, but instead be dressed – should that be draped? – in a Grecian tunic and to wear a pair of handmade leather sandals in order that as much fresh air as possible would be able to circulate freely about her person.

Unfortunately these strictures continued well into Maria's adulthood so that when she was married and pregnant she was still receiving parental instructions to drink only water which had been boiled up with pine-needles and to ensure that every tree in the vicinity of her house had been culled in order to prevent her picking up something unpleasant from the bark. Madame also recommended that she never, ever travelled when the wind was coming from the east – although the reason for this was never made entirely clear.

Despite her bossiness in such matters it was frequently suspected that the Comtesse herself never actually ate the mutton she recommended so forcefully. This was because a screen was always placed around her at mealtimes lending support to the theory that while her guests struggled through their greasy stew Madame was busy dipping into something far more toothsome.

The milk thing was certainly for real though, and she stuck with that until the end of her days. Family picnic excursions, for example, would always be accompanied by a cow or two which would be milked directly into glasses before these were topped up with cognac. In later life she lived almost entirely on milk and champagne, a perfectly disgusting-sounding combination, although she must have got something right because she lived until she was eighty-four.

She left a fortune when she died, but also – alas – a dozen different wills, each containing different plans for the disposal of an estimated £100,000. Fortunately all of these agreed on one central point: that Maria should get the bulk of it but solely on condition that she dressed in white every day throughout the summer and never, ever laced-up her shoes.

Northamptonshire

DEENE PARK, nr Corby

At various times the Countess of Cardigan, Condessa de Lancastre and finally Countess of Lancaster (when she mischievously encouraged the Anglicisation of her Portuguese title), when the former Miss Adeline Louisa Maria de Horsey (1825–1915) wasn't busy rehearsing her death by lying-in-state at Deene she displayed a tiresomely, teenager-like determination to offend others by behaving badly.

Of course in Victorian society this was not so hard to do, and today one is inclined to smile at the idea that anyone might be seriously outraged by Adeline smoking cigarettes in public or daring to go out on a bicycle dressed in a her husband's old regimental trousers. But she knew exactly what she was up to, and would also have known that far from being hers, the title 'Countess of Lancaster' belonged to the Sovereign and at this time was one of Queen Victoria's preferred pseudonyms when she wished to travel around her realm in secret.

Picking a fight with a monarch was of course far from clever, but in Adeline's opinion the fault lay with Queen Victoria who she insisted had kick-started hostilities in the first place by refusing ever to forgive her for living in sin with the 7th Earl of Cardigan. The two had lived this way for a year before marrying, compounding what in the 1850s was a considerable offence against social mores by letting it be widely known that their affair had started while the Earl's first wife was still busy dying.

When they did marry the Queen's response was to refuse to receive Adeline at court, a considerable a snub for anyone let alone the young wife of the hero of Balaclava. It clearly rankled too, for when Adeline married for a second time in 1873, this time to the Portuguese Don Antonio Manuel de Lancastere Soldana, Conde de Lancastre, she saw immediately that by adapting her new title to its more English-sounding equivalent she could have some small revenge on the Queen.

(In 1909 the offence was further reinforced when her autobiography, *My Recollections*, was credited to 'Adeline Louisa Maria de Horsey Cardigan and Lancaster' even though strictly speaking she was forbidden by the complex rules governing the British peerages to join titles together in this way.)

Perhaps as a result of her being barred from official entertainments she organised her own at Deene Park, and rapidly became one of the unelected leaders of a somewhat 'fast' set – in London as well as the shires – a position she continued to hold into old age.

Mostly dividing her time between the capital and the ancestral seat of the Cardigans (which she had somehow retained even after her remarriage) she continued to scandalise public opinion until well into her dotage by wearing particularly heavy make-up and organising steeplechases which were run through the middle of the local graveyard.

Soirées at Deene tended to follow a somewhat eccentric course, with her ladyship on occasion dressing up in an Iberian flamenco style to entertain her guests – something she was still doing when she was well into her eighties – and demanding that everyone pretend to faint when she appeared after dinner dressed as a nun. (Although she had long insisted that Deene Park was haunted by the ghost of a nun, this was apparently her idea of a joke rather than a genuine attempt to persuade people that the ghost was real.)

Lady Lancastre also kept an open coffin in the ballroom at Deene, her own, and aided by her butler would climb in and out of it on a regular basis in order to reassure herself that it was still a good fit and still comfortable enough to last her into the next world. Whenever she felt the need to do this, which was apparently often, the rest of the household would be required to attend and afterwards be invited to give an opinion as to how her final send-off might be improved.

Unfortunately while continuing to live in the Earl's ancestral home after her marriage to the Portuguese count – Lord Cardigan had died after a fall from a horse, and as they had no children the title went to a cousin – she had access to the Cardigan fortune which soon collapsed

under the weight of her extravagant lifestyle. Much of her distinctive apparel was thus sold off when she was made bankrupt, although as an old lady she would still attend the local meets in full hunting-dress even though by this time it was her practice to arrive by coach, affect to believe that her groom had delivered her horse to the wrong place, and then settle down merely to observe.

EASTON NESTON, nr Towcester

With automobiles in the early days accused of doing little more than scaring the horses it was perhaps only natural that the aristocracy – traditionally hippophilic and deeply conservative – should take a general dislike to the things initially.

Pioneering motorists ('motorious carbarians' in the words of *The Times*) were portrayed as selfish, reckless and intolerably arrogant. Few noblemen went so far as Percy Sholto Douglas, 10th Marquess of Queensberry – who sought the courts' permission to shoot dead any and all motorists on the grounds that simply by existing they endangered the lives of his family – but plenty saw in the motor car a direct assault on the natural order they had enjoyed for generations.

Of course there were exceptions. In 1903 the bigamous Earl Russell queued all night to get 'A1', the world's first ever numberplate. Two years later Charles Chetwynd-Talbot, otherwise the 23rd Lord Shrewsbury, allowed a make of motor car to be named after him, and Lord Kitchener – clearly no shrinking violet – had his Rolls-Royce painted bright yellow so people would recognise him being driven around town and ensure him right of way.

A few peers entered the fray as racing drivers too, such as the Le Mans-winning Earl Howe in the 1920s (apparently he took it up at the suggestion of a magistrate who was tired of fining him for speeding) and more recently the Jaguar-driving Johnny Dumfries who won the 1988 race but is these days more correctly known as the 7th Marquess of Bute.

Dumfries had earlier enjoyed a brief career in Formula One as well, after joining Lotus for a single season as the great Ayrton Senna's team-mate. In this particular arena though, his contribution has perhaps been overshadowed by that of Thomas Alexander Fermor-Hesketh, 3rd Baron Hesketh, who sooner than climb into someone else's car started his own Formula One team from scratch – as well as later trying single-handedly to revive the British motorcycle industry.

HESKETH F1

Today his efforts in both fields might look eccentric, not least because by the 1970s F1 was already a very high-stakes game in which even the biggest players relied on sponsorship from major multinationals in order to pay the bills. Japanese domination was similarly almost total when it came to big bikes.

Hesketh was having none of it, however, refusing all corporate sponsorship for his beloved F1 team – powered by patriotism, the cars were red, white and blue and plain but for a cute teddy bear logo – and developing the cars (and later his all-new all-British superbike) in buildings on the family estate at Easton Neston.

It is tempting to suppose that both ventures were always bound to fail. In due course they did so, but not before leaving their mark and winning huge plaudits from the public who recognised and admired his lordship's courageous if quixotic enthusiasm – and not inconsiderable expertise.

But neither scheme was remotely amateur, although the commitment to having a good time and a certain extravagance meant the F1 team – and in particular its star driver James Hunt – was frequently viewed as something of a playboy exercise, with Rolls-Royces arriving in the paddock at party time, and plenty of champagne for anyone who wanted it.

Hunt was a drinker but no fool, however, and while his victory in the World Drivers' Championship was still a while away his time at Hesketh saw the team score several impressive podium places in its debut 1973 season. The following year was better still, and the 1975 Dutch Grand Prix is still remembered for the way in which the Englishman managed to hold off Niki Lauda's superior Ferrari

in horrendous weather on his way to scoring the first British
grand prix victory in years – and the last one ever by a privately funded
team.

Following Hunt's departure to a stronger rival the Bunterish Hesketh
withdrew, but keen to use the skills, personnel and facilities he had
established at Easton, he decided to have a go at building a new big
bike. The first V-Twin V1000 was up and running around the estate by
1980, a handsome machine which was also the first British bike to have
four valves per cylinder and twin overhead camshafts.

A couple of years later an impressive purpose-built factory was
opened at nearby Daventry, and a new company registered under
the name of Hesketh Motorcycles plc. Unfortunately it soon became
apparent that there was insufficient cash to take on the might of
the Japanese, and while there were certainly British bikers out there
who wanted to ride British bikes, several much bigger names, such
as Norton and Triumph, were also having a hard time staying in
business.

Sadly Hesketh was eventually forced to call it a day, by which time
fewer than 140 bikes had been built and sold making them rare and
sought-after machines today. Without Lord Hesketh, and under
new management, a more advanced Hesketh Vampire continued in
production back at Easton until 2006. By then the Hawksmoor pile had
been sold to a Russian-born Californian fashion mogul, bringing to a
close nearly 350 years of Fermor-Hesketh occupancy.

RUSHTON LODGE, Rushton Hall, nr Rothwell (EH)

The famous Triangular Lodge at Rushton Hall is one of the strangest
buildings in England, and also among the most dangerous. It is the
creation of Sir Thomas Tresham (1545–1605), the head of a leading
Catholic family with a decided penchant for tweaking the tail of the
Establishment at a time when the Protestant authorities were adept at
biting back and clearly happy to do so as viciously as possible.

Perhaps the clearest case of this was his son Sir Francis (1567–
1605) who joined with the Earl of Essex in his miserably unsuccessful
rebellion of 1601, and when that failed to unseat Elizabeth soon
afterwards became embroiled in the Gunpowder Plotters' attempt to
kill her successor King James I.

On the first occasion family connections and his father's money were
sufficient to save him from being attainted though poor old Essex was

executed for his folly. But in 1605 Sir Francis was less fortunate, his father dead, the money running out, he died in the Tower of London, probably of a urinary infection just days ahead of his own execution for treason.

The estate at Rushton then passed to his brother together with the aforementioned Triangular Lodge, although had the latter been fully recognised at the time for what it was, it seems likely that none of the Treshams would ever have seen the place again.

English Heritage call the little lodge 'delightful', as indeed it is. It is also a rather more distinguished structure than the hall itself, which was converted into a school in the 1950s and is now an hotel. More than this though, it is a statement of the Treshams' Roman Catholic faith, Sir Thomas having designed it to incorporate as many references as possible to the Holy Trinity despite the obvious danger to his personal wellbeing.

Once you know this, the clues are everywhere. Most obviously it is triangular. There are also three floors, three triangular gables on each of the three façades, and three windows on each floor of each façade, some of these decorative trefoils containing patterns of yet more triangles. An inscription over the entrance continues the theme – *TRES TESTIMONIUM DANT*, a quotation from John's Gospel meaning 'there are three that bear witness'– while there is also a triangular chimney on top of it, and down below three more Latin texts each of which runs to exactly 33 characters.

Essentially useless the principal rooms inside are hexagonal, meaning there are plenty more triangles, with one in the corner of each of the three floors, while throughout the building one finds numerous clues to the Elizabethans' love of allegory and numerology.

Above the main door, for example, is carved '5555'. Subtract from that 1593 – the year Tresham is known to have begun work on his folly – and one is left with 3958, the date (BC) of the Deluge, according to the calculations of the Venerable Bede. Elsewhere, similarly, one finds '3509' and '3898' carved, respectively the dates for the Creation and the Call of Abraham when the Patriarch 'was called to go out into a place which he should after receive for an inheritance, obeyed; and he went out, not knowing whether he went.'

At one level of course the building can be seen as little more than an ingenious game, a rich man's plaything notwithstanding that by the time Sir Thomas died the whole estate was in reality hugely indebted. But it was also a proclamation of an unswerving but at the time highly dangerous belief, a blatant advertisement for the faith and passion which were to cost Sir Thomas so dear. In his lifetime, as a convert, he was fined a total of £8,000 for being a Catholic, equivalent to more than £10,000,000 today; at other times he found himself held hostage whenever the machinations of Catholics overseas were held to be menacing the safety of the realm. Ultimately that same faith was to cost his son his life, making the Triangular Lodge as tragic as it is whimsical, and not a little eccentric at a time when Catholics might have been better advised to lie low and bide their time.

Northumberland

A builder but also a destroyer – much of his vast wealth was built on weapons manufacture – the enormous home of William Armstrong, 1st and last Baron Armstrong, says much about the man. Like the best kind of Victorian industrial magnate he built a fortune from nothing, and perhaps carried away by the scale of his achievements came genuinely to believe that with sufficient money, determination and sheer willpower man could harness and tame anything, even Nature herself.

How else to explain his decision to build here? On nearly 3 square miles of wild, windswept Northumbria, a bare, rocky hillside which was to be transformed by planting more than seven million trees – some of them reputed to be the highest in England – he chose a location so remote from the surrounding population that the most practical way of getting electricity into the house turned out to be to generate it himself on site.

Armstrong had no family but everything about the place was nevertheless built to the largest possible scale, from the more than 30 miles of driveways around the estate to the five artificial lakes. Then of course there was the house itself which incorporated a riotous confusion of Jacobean, Tudor, Rhenish and Gothic styles blended together by the prolific architect (of London's Bedford Park and New Scotland Yard) Richard Norman Shaw. Over a period of fifteen years the influential Norman Shaw extended a small lodge into a mammoth country house, freely mixing Elizabethan mullions with Ludwig of Bavaria fairytale towers, and cosy, domestic pre-Raphaelite decoration and detailing with the very latest in novel and advanced technology.

The latter was perhaps unsurprising: in a long working life (he died in harness, aged ninety) Armstrong combined his training as a lawyer and inventing engineer to create an international manufacturing conglomerate that churned out engines, cranes, waterworks and warships for the Empire and beyond – as well as the armaments which were to see him cited as the model for George Bernard Shaw's *Major Barbara*.

A painting commissioned at the time shows the great man in slippers with his little dog, reading peacefully by the fireside, but it is hard to imagine a man like Armstrong ever taking it easy, and the likelihood is

there was nothing quiet or retiring about life at Cragside whenever he was at home.

The first house in the world to be lit by hydroelectric power, hence the five lakes, Armstrong also used this innovative power source to drive a battery of fantastic domestic machines. Spits in the kitchen were automatically turned, while heavy pans were mechanically lowered down to the scullery to be washed and brought back up. The greenhouses were similarly well provided for, Cragside's over-abundance of home-made electricity being used to turn the pots each morning, afternoon and evening in order that Armstrong's plants would continue to face toward the sun. Elsewhere on the estate, water power was employed to run threshing and winnowing machinery, and even a private saw mill.

Lord Armstrong was also among the first country house owners to fit hundreds of new electric carbon-filament lamps, which were certainly brighter than traditional gas mantles but also liable to ignite spontaneously so that weekend guests at Cragside were routinely provided with cushions to stifle any flames. (Mind you, even this must have represented a considerable advance over two other lights at the house which switched themselves on automatically, but only if placed in a bowl of mercury. Switching them off was guaranteed to result in an electric shock for the unfortunate servant, and then of course there was the matter of the mercury fumes . . .)

In Armstrong's own lifetime visitors flocked to witness such marvels for themselves, Cragside's dishwasher, Turkish bath and hot and cold running water quickly seeing the place dubbed 'the palace of a modern magician'. Such guests included not only honoured customers from overseas – the company he founded supplied military equipment to many friendly powers (and as Vickers it continued to do so until 2004) – but also the Prince and Princess of Wales, who stayed in the 1880s, the Shah of Persia, the King of Siam, Afghanistan's Crown Prince and the Chinese Prime Minister. No US presidents, however, perhaps because throughout the 1860s Lord Armstrong had been quietly supplying both sides in the Civil War.

Sadly of course what one generation builds up is often left to the next to knock down, and while Cragside survived, Armstrong's fortune was to be dispersed in considerably less time than it had taken to build. A small portion went to found the University of Newcastle, and to rebuild the city's Royal Victoria Infirmary and the Hancock Natural History Museum, but having inherited £1.4 million from his great uncle in 1900 – a figure one could multiply by several hundred today – William Watson-Armstrong had sold most of Armstrong's considerable art collection within a decade and surrendered the house to the National Trust.

Nottinghamshire

BESTWOOD LODGE, nr Arnold

They used to call this part of the county the Dukeries, and with good reason. Close by Worksop no fewer than four ducal seats cluster together – Clumber Park (the Dukes of Newcastle), Thoresby Hall (Kingston), Welbeck Abbey (Portland) and Worksop Manor (Norfolk) – and only a few miles away is Bestwood Lodge, built for the 10th Duke of St Albans in the English Gothic Revival style by S.S. Teulon.

Now an hotel, Bestwood is by no means the most impressive ducal seat in the country (or even the county) but then neither have the St Albans been the most illustrious or distinguished of dukes. Famously descended from Nell Gwyn – and as such one of five surviving dukedoms pressed on the mistresses of Charles II – some have indeed been perfectly respectable, but others were perfectly mad.

The 3rd Duke was nicknamed the Simple Duke after a life characterised by one biographer as 'a glittering crescendo of feats of incompetence'. The 6th was described as 'the most hideous, disagreeable little animal' by one of his own set, while the 9th caused a scandal by seducing a housemaid and then marrying some distance beneath him. (His bride was an Irishwoman called Gubbins, who is sometimes thought to have brought insanity into the family although in this regard at least they seemed fairly well set up already.)

Certainly things got even worse afterwards, with the 11th Duke briefly captaining the South Nottinghamshire Yeomanry but then being required to spend the last thirty years of his life in a secure clinic in Sussex. His brother joined him shortly afterwards, having mounted a pretty serious attempt at burning down his old school, Eton College.

The death of the 11th Duke in 1934 left the way open for a half-brother Osborne de Vere Beauclerk. He became 12th Duke of St Albans, Earl of Burford, Baron Vere of Hanworth and of Heddington (1875–1964) – but always 'Obby' to his pals – with his succession eliciting a sigh of relief from the family as he was merely a tad odd in his habits rather than actually clinically insane.

That said, and like a few latter-day dukes, Obby made it clear pretty early on that he wished to play as small a part as possible in public life. In 1953 for example he decided to boycott the Queen's coronation when as Hereditary Grand Falconer of England he was refused permission to attend with a live falcon on his arm. (Palace officials tactfully suggested he wear a stuffed bird instead, but he wasn't having any of that.)

In a family famous for remaining childless he left it late to get married too, becoming engaged to Beatrix Beresford, Dowager Marchioness of Waterford at the age of forty-three. She had half a dozen children already, and Obby wisely decided to leave it at that just in case the aforementioned insanity was actually hereditary. (Bizarrely he had no such qualms about illegitimate offspring, however, and left so many of these that he was reportedly never entirely sure who many of them were or how many he had.)

With Bestwood already gone the usual way of the St Albans fortune – the buyer was the founder of the Raleigh Bicycle Company (see Thame Park, p. 126) – Obby spent much of his time in Ireland. There he gained a reputation for interrupting the sermon each Sunday by periodically shouting 'rubbish!' from underneath the handkerchief with which for some reason he liked to conceal his face while catching forty winks. Occasionally he would visit London in order to drop into the Turf Club or Brooks's in St James's Street – where Newman, the hall porter, was expected to wind his watch for him on the way in – and then suddenly in 1958, at the age of eighty-three, he decided to change the habit of a lifetime and hit the road for real.

When he did this his choice of destination – the Americas – was perhaps less surprising than his chosen modes of travel: a rough and ready cabin aboard a freighter crossing the Atlantic, followed by a Greyhound bus which he rode from coast to coast. The Americans clearly loved the idea of a gen-u-wine English lord slumming it in this way, and he reportedly received no fewer than sixty-eight proposals of marriage before setting off to explore South America. This he did by second-class train, presumably by this time recognising the reality that such was the state of the Beauclerk fortune that when the time came for his heir to inherit he would get a string of titles but little if anything else.

BUNNY HALL, Bunny, nr Nottingham

The most spectacular funerary monuments in English churches tend to be among the most boastful, aspirational types, seeming as a rule to prefer display to reticence and rarely missing an opportunity to demonstrate or document the achievements of the dead.

A rare exception is Sir Thomas Parkyns (1663–1741) a lawyer and Latin scholar who, while by no means unimpressive in his

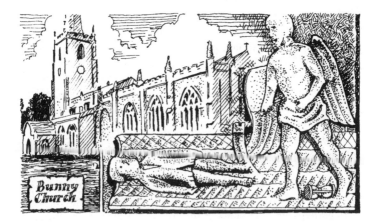

Bunny Church

achievements, commissioned a monument for his local church depicting him lying prostrate on the floor having lost a wrestling bout with a figure representing Father Time.

Next to this is another full size effigy, showing him squaring up for a fight. Sir Thomas, it transpires, was another battling baronet – albeit with a slightly more scholarly bent than the aforementioned Sir Claude Champion De Crespigny. Sir Claude, one suspects, would clearly have sooner fought than write about it, while Sir Thomas – though as keen to get stuck in – was such a passionate advocate of the noble art of wrestling that he also spent a good deal of time drafting a treatise on what was known as 'Inn Play' or Cornish Hugg Wrestling, 'a method which teacheth to break holds, and throw most falls mathematically'.

This was published at his own expense in 1713, and dedicated to George I, by which time Sir Thomas was also employing two full-time wrestlers at Bunny Hall to supervise his annual wrestling contest. Anyone in the area who wished to partake could do so, the prize being a lace-trimmed hat worth 22s with a 3s consolation prize for the runner-up. On a number of occasions he was thrown to the ground by his own servants, and it must say something for the man that this never seemed to bother him unduly.

Wrestling was by no means his only eccentricity, however, as he also collected stone coffins – many more of them than he could ever have used – and as a skilled if amateur architect spent a great deal of time 'contriving and drawing all his own plans' for a number of buildings in the village which was one of several he owned in the area.

His most ambitious plans he kept for the hall, however, adding an extraordinary brick wing to the existing house. This is crowned by a bizarre castellated tower mounted on top of an immense – and it should be said, slightly awkward – curved pediment. The slightly theatrical effect of this has been compared (mostly unfavourably) with the work of Sir John Vanbrugh at Castle Howard and Claremont in Surrey, but the work is cruder and much clumsier with a preponderance of strange detailing, including a pair of wholly unneccessary buttresses, what look like a pair of sentry boxes and an absurdly large representation of its creator's coat of arms.

That said, even with its blind windows, the 60ft tower would have functioned perfectly well as a belvedere to look out over the surrounding deer park, and of course at Bunny Hall Sir Thomas was attempting to create something entirely novel – most eighteenth-century gentleman-amateurs managed perfectly well without an indoor wrestling arena – so perhaps one should not be too critical of the finished result and instead applaud his originality.

CLUMBER PARK, nr Worksop (NT)

These days one is accustomed to family fortunes being managed by independent trustees. Often this is done in a (perfectly legal) bid to minimise the tax burden which might otherwise lead to the break-up of great and historic estates. Occasionally, however, it depends on parents or grandparents who are far-sighted enough to realise that a particular heir may not have the skills or the temperament needed to maintain or improve an inheritance which has taken literally centuries to accumulate.

In fact such a scenario is far from new, and it is now more than a century and a half since such steps were taken to ensure that Clumber Park – and the attendant fortune that had taken three Earls of Clare and five Dukes of Newcastle several hundred years to amass – was not going to be lost at the gaming tables by young Henry Pelham Alexander Pelham-Clinton (1834–79) once he became the 6th Duke of Newcastle.

The trustees appointed by his grandfather were right to be concerned. Known as Lord Clinton until 1851 and then Lord Lincoln before he inherited the dukedom in 1864, the Old Etonian and Oxford-educated Pelham-Clinton was very briefly MP for Newark but in a relatively short life did little but gamble unsuccessfully and made no attempt – besides marrying a rich heiress – to make good his losses.

Very much a Victorian gentleman but with a Regency taste for high living, by the age of twenty-five the feckless, frivolous playboy was so indebted that he was forced to leave the country as he had no way of paying his creditors. By 1860 he is thought to have been £230,000 in the red. Today an equivalent sum would be around £150 million based on average earnings (or a mere £16 million using the retail price index) and certainly it would not have helped that as a Pelham-Clinton the future Duke would have been more or less guaranteed membership of White's in London. Today's members like to think of their elegant clubhouse as an oasis of civilisation in a desert of democracy, but in truth Edward Harley, 2nd Earl of Oxford, was probably nearer the mark when he described it as place where 'young noblemen were fleeced and corrupted by fashionable gamblers and profligates'.

Pelham-Clinton certainly found out the hard way what went on at 37 St James's Street, but soon after going into self-imposed exile he was fortunate enough to meet Henrietta Adela Hope. She was the daughter and heiress of the immensely wealthy chairman of the Eastern Steam Navigation Company, owner of Brunel's magnificent 'Great Babe', the SS *Great Eastern*.

S.S. GREAT EASTERN

Described at the time as illegitimate but pretty – reportedly true on both counts – she was to be the duke's salvation. As well as being the Hope after whom the fabulous 'Hope Diamond' was named, she was assured of an income of at least £50,000 a year once she had married and settled Pelham-Clinton's debts. Of course Henry Hope was no fool, and while keen to see his daughter marry so well he had taken legal steps to ensure that the estates he settled on the couple – in Surrey,

Gloucestershire, the Midlands and Ireland – were there to be enjoyed but would remain administratively out of reach of the new Duke.

For a while it worked, not least one suspects because the 6th Duke was very soon replaced by a slightly less useless 7th. But sadly both family and fortune were destined to be ruined in the end. In 1912 the great mansion at Clumber was destroyed in a fire (it was rebuilt, but then torn down again in the 1930s.) The Newcastle title went too, devolved to a bachelor and after his death disappearing into extinction. And following a number of well-publicised auctions – the diamond went for the equivalent of £2 million and is now in New York's Smithsonian Institution, and another sale shifted 9 tons of valuable antique books – the remains of Clumber Park passed into the safer care of the National Trust.

WELBECK ABBEY, nr Worksop

A formidable builder, and more pertinently Britain's foremost human mole, William John Cavendish, the reclusive 5th Duke of Portland (1800–79) was at one time said to have employed 15,000 workers building above and below ground on his Welbeck Abbey estate.

His creations included an underground ballroom and three different libraries, all of them painted pink, the Duke famously giving each of the workers and tenants an umbrella and a donkey on the understanding that they never spoke to him or doffed their caps. All ducal instructions were issued to staff in writing, the principal rooms at Welbeck being fitted with two letterboxes, one for incoming and the other for outgoing missives. Anyone encountering His Grace in the park at Welbeck was similarly instructed to pass by him 'as they would a tree'.

At one point His Grace is said to have considered building a tunnel so he could travel unobserved to Worksop station more than 3 miles away, and he is known to have twice refused the Order of the Garter because accepting it would have required him to put in an appearance at Court.

Indeed such was his abhorrence of appearing in public that after his accession to the dukedom it took a full three years for him to take up his seat in the House of Lords. In part at least this might have been because he was kept busy at Welbeck, stripping all the rooms of their furniture, carpets, pictures and wall-hangings – fortunately these were stored rather than sold although why he did it is still a mystery – and moving into a suite of just four or five rooms in the west wing.

The Duke also instructed his staff, presumably by letter, to order hundreds of gallons of pink paint to paint every inch of wall, sufficient wig boxes to fill an entire room (all coloured green, and each containing a wig) and – according to his socialite cousin Lady Ottoline Morrell – insisting that commodes be fitted in every one of the scores of rooms he had recently vacated. The kitchens at Welbeck were also required to have at least one chicken roasting at every hour of the day, just in case His Grace felt needful of a snack.

Mostly though he was interesting in digging and, with an army of several hundred Irish navvies imported for the task, he set about creating a vast complex of subterranean spaces including the aforementioned ballroom – at 160ft by 64ft large enough to accommodate 2,000 revellers – together with a 250ft long library, a vast, glass-roofed observatory and one of the largest billiard rooms ever seen with room for perhaps half a dozen tables.

Putting all this underground was strange enough, but it was doubly so for a man who recoiled from the idea of entertaining others at home. Similarly the Duke kept 100 horses stabled (with 45 grooms on standby) even though he was never known to ride, and constructed a vast new indoor riding school – nearly 400ft long and 110ft wide, it was lit by 8,000 individual gas jets – that almost certainly remained unused until after his death.

In all no fewer than eight tunnels were excavated beneath the estate, totalling between 3 and 15 miles depending on whom you listen to, while at his Cavendish Square house in London he had an extraordinary 80ft high frosted glass screen erected around the garden in order to prevent anyone catching a glimpse of him promenading around the lawn.

Here and at home in Nottinghamshire His Grace would habitually sport a minimum of two overcoats, together with a 2ft high top hat, and trouser-legs held a few inches above his ankle by knotted string. Always seen with an umbrella (useful to hide behind should anyone attempt to start a conversation) he would order three coats at a time in different sizes so that one would fit snugly inside another in the manner of a Russian doll.

Though highly reclusive, he was said to hold a candle for the singer Adelaide Kemble, but it will surprise no-one to learn that the Duke died unmarried. Described after this death as 'vast, splendid and utterly comfortless' Welbeck Abbey with his eccentric additions is still intact, however, and with the pink now painted over, served until 2005 as an Army staff college. Descendants of the 7th Duke still own the estate and live there, but not in the abbey. With the dukedom now extinct its future use is unknown.

Oxfordshire

FARINGDON HOUSE, Faringdon

Maintaining the aristocracy's record of rampant eccentricity until well into the twentieth century, Gerald Hugh Tyrwhitt-Wilson 14th Baron Berners (1883–1950) invited a horse to afternoon tea and liked to dye the pigeons on his estate a variety of bright colours. Taking care to use a dye that did them no harm, and with an occasional penchant for monochromatic meals – his fellow composer Stravinsky reported that 'if his mood was pink, lunch might consist of beet soup, lobster, tomatoes, strawberries' – he would have the birds repeatedly redyed to match whatever he was planning to eat.

Short, witty and highly musical, his lordship went to the trouble of having a piano keyboard installed in the back of his Rolls-Royce, enabling him to compose on the move, and as a lifelong bachelor bought diamond-studded collars for his adored pet whippets.

Despite such exertions on his part – not to mention a busy professional life as a diplomat, bon viveur and writer – it was his passion for building which really put Berners on the map, particularly when a distant but vociferous neighbour objected at length to his plans to build an isolated 104ft folly of his own design on a corner of his Faringdon estate.

The gentleman in question, one Admiral Clifton-Browne, reportedly objected to this on the grounds that the tower would his view. When Berners suggested that Clifton-Browne would obscure be able to see

his tower only with the aid of a telescope, the old sea-dog indignantly pointed out that being a retired admiral he rarely looked at the world through anything else. Capt. Salty went to court to prove it too, but the court found for Berners and when the tower was completed the joyful owner put up a sign warning that 'Members Of The Public Committing Suicide From This Tower Do So At Their Own Risk'.

Elsewhere around the estate were other signs warning that stray dogs would be shot and cats whipped, and while far from reclusive Lord Berners was also known to go to great lengths to secure a private compartment when travelling by train. Here his most successful ruse involved donning dark glasses and a black skullcap before leaning out of the window and beckoning passers-by to join him. If this didn't work (and probably it did most of the time) he would pull out a giant thermometer and with an increasingly distressed expression proceed every few minutes to take his temperature until anyone who dared to sit anywhere near him eventually stood up and moved on.

FRIAR PARK, nr Henley

For many years home to the late musician and keen gardener George Harrison, Friar Park was largely the creation of solicitor Sir Frank Crisp (1843–1919). With a diverse list of clients ranging from the Liberal Party in its heyday to the Imperial Japanese Navy, Sir Frank was also responsible for drafting the contract when it came to cutting the fabulous Cullinan diamond. Like many high-achievers he pursued his hobbies with unusual vigour, becoming a founder member of the Royal Microscopical Society and such an obsessively enthusiastic horticulturalist that work started on the gardens at Friar Park before the foundations for his huge French Gothic house had even been dug.

Inevitably his plans included many rare species and a few follies, although the towers and turrets were largely restricted to the house. Outside the centrepiece was the Alpine Garden, reputed at the time to be the largest rockery in the world, built using more than 7,000 tons of millstone grit which Sir Frank and his gardener Philip Knowles brought down from Yorkshire. This incorporated a scale model of the Matterhorn which was more than 20ft tall and with the summit carved from a piece of rock from the actual mountain. On its lower slopes grazed cast iron replicas of gazelles and the spot was carefully marked where four English mountaineers fell to their deaths in 1865. Such was Sir Frank's devotion to accuracy that the mountain had to be pulled down and rebuilt several times by uncomplaining workmen before its new owner was finally satisfied.

In fact such things were not entirely unknown, and around this same time a replica Mount Fuji was built on another estate in Hertfordshire, and a model of the Khyber Pass in East Park, Hull. Sir Frank was anyway probably even more interested in what went on below ground level than above it as he commissioned a London firm of specialists to excavate and decorate a series of caverns beneath his 42-acre gardens. Variously called the Blue Grotto, Ice Grotto, Vine Grotto, Wishing Well Cave and so on, these were interlinked and cunningly electrified so that guests could pass through from one to another and enjoy such delights as a model crocodile with illuminated eyes, and a Chinese stork which appeared to drink. Elsewhere skeletons automatically launched themselves at passers-by, faces stared up from beneath the waters, and amid a clutch of snuff-taking gnomes, some kind of mechanically induced underground rainbow illuminated the Stygian gloom.

When the house was built it too included several similarly curious touches, including model friars in many of the rooms whose noses had to be turned in order to switch on the lights. The aforementioned Lady Ottoline Morrell was unable to decide after visiting in 1905 whether Friar Park's owner was actually so simple as to think 'these vulgar and monstrous jokes beautiful and amusing' – but more than a century later it sounds like delightful whimsy.

In his time Sir Frank was happy to show guests round, and did so frequently. Privately though he called them IVs – 'ignorant visitors' – and took care to warn them not to offend his staff by being rude about the gardens or anything found there while walking around. He insisted that 'every care is taken to secure as gardeners men of placid temperament and not given to outbursts of feeling. But exceptions will sometimes creep in, and the owner cannot therefore always be responsible for consequences.'

Some time following his death in 1919 Friar Park fell on hard times with the gardens gradually decaying under the ownership of the Order of St John Bosco. Remodelling the house as a school the brothers will have had limited if any use for caverns and model mountains, but fortunately in 1969 Friar Park caught the eye of a sensitive new owner who set about putting things right. George Harrison also chose to commemorate the gardens' creator in a typically engaging song 'Ballad of Sir Frankie Crisp (Let it Roll)' which appeared on his first post-Beatles release, the highly influential triple-album *All Things Must Pass*.

SWINBROOK HOUSE, Swinbrook, nr Burford

Perhaps the most celebrated family of eccentrics of the twentieth century, the fame of the Mitford sisters may have eclipsed that of their father but there seems little doubt that any peculiarities the girls may have displayed in later life had their origins in their upbringing under the stern and somewhat gimlet eye of their father.

The sisters' friend Evelyn Waugh affixed a brass plate to his gate pillars reading 'No Admittance on Business' in order to ward off the uninvited, and was famously testy. He nevertheless exuded warmth and welcome when compared to the Mitfords' father, David Bertram Ogilvy Freeman Mitford, 2nd Baron Redesdale (1878–1958), who sought to exclude pretty much everyone from his world and did so at every possible opportunity.

'Farve', as he was known, absolutely hated what he called outsiders, the term very much a blanket description which came to include not just foreigners of any stripe but all children other than his own, and any of his own children's friends especially if they were male. Nancy Mitford's In Pursuit of Love parodied this stance wonderfully ('Frogs are slightly better than Huns or Wops, but abroad is unutterably bloody and foreigners are fiends') but in reality the old misery was even worse. He never bothered to differentiate between one foreigner and another, for example, and when his nephew married an Argentinian girl of Spanish descent he affected to believe she was black.

From the start his mistrust of 'outsiders' was such that he personally supervised the births of all seven of his children, on the first such occasion so taking against the doctor's methods that, in his own words, 'I seized him by the neck and shook him like a rat.' The vicar was treated with equal disdain, if a bit less violence. Warning him off sermons of more than ten minutes ('If you disregard this I shall precipitate you out of the pulpit by the scruff of the neck!') Redesdale also made it clear that he wanted 'none of those damn' complicated foreign tunes' and that in selecting the hymns each Sunday the selection should be restricted to the likes of 'Rock of Ages' and 'All Things Bright and Beautiful'.

Redesdale, in short, was a bully, although in the manner of a more deferential age his obituary in The Times in 1958 described him merely as someone 'who adhered to somewhat old-fashioned views with tenacity and boisterousness.' If nothing else he is proof, were it needed, that eccentrics are recognised only from a distance or in retrospect, and that any closer association would see a majority of them instantly reclassified instead as obnoxious, insufferable and not infrequently completely idiotic.

As a child too thick to be considered for Eton, Redesdale was subsequently unable to pass the entrance examination into Sandhurst although, despite losing a lung, he fought with distinction in both the Boer War and the First World War. Thereafter his ignorance seems to have become something of a badge of honour, and he liked to brag that despite having four of his six daughters go on to become highly regarded authors, he had only ever read one book in his entire life and it was not by any of them.

The boast was also something of an odd one for a man who had married into a publishing family, but was perhaps borne out by Redesdale's less than successful time at the helm of *The Lady* magazine, which had been started by his wife's father and is still owned by the family.

Despite his utter distrust of foreigners, Redesdale somehow conceived a measure of admiration for Hitler and (quick to voice extreme right-wing and anti-Semitic views) he was, according to his daughter Diana, 'a natural fascist'. Once war was declared, however, he pretty quickly changed his mind, his previously strong opinions swamped by a dose of fairly naked patriotism and then overwhelmed entirely when his son Tom was killed in action.

The death of his heir affected him greatly, and for much of the remainder of his life Lord Redesdale withdrew to Inch Kenneth – a small island he had bought off the west coast of Scotland – and later to the Northumberland village of Redesdale. He died a virtual recluse, with nary an outsider to bother him.

THAME PARK, Thame

For 400 years a Cistercian Abbey, and more recently the unlikely setting for a number of scenes in the movie *Saving Private Ryan*, for nearly four decades Thame Park was home to the colourful Sir Frank Bowden, Bt (1909–2001) described by his obiturist in the *Daily Telegraph* as a ninety-two-year-old 'cheetah-owning collector of Japanese swords and armour.'

The money to indulge these passions came from industry, Sir Frank being the grandson of another Sir Frank who had built a fortune on the foundation of the Raleigh Bicycle Company. The 1st Baronet had become interested in cycling only when doctors gave him a few months to live, succeeding in beating the odds and seeing his little workshop grow into the industrial behemoth which subsequently swallowed up many of its suppliers and rivals including Triumph, Sturmey-Archer, Humber, Rudge-Whitworth and BSA.

By 1938 the company spread over more than 20 acres and was selling more than 2,000,000 machines annually. The younger Sir Frank was even so more interested in military power than pedal power and he began to fill Thame Park with what might well have been the world's largest private collection of swords, spears, halberds and 'sleeve entanglers' – a kind of dangerously spiked pole.

His interest in such things had originally been fired when he inherited several weapons from his grandfather, although his personal taste tended towards the Oriental taking in everything from the great thirteenth-century swordsmith Ichimonji Norifusa of Bizen to the style of weapon issued to Japanese officers in the Second World War. One of the latter was acquired for his collection complete with a note confirming that the blade had been independently tested on a malefactor's neck, and in time his interest in Japan led him to become president of the Kendo Society and a vice-president of the Japan Society for which he was awarded the Order of the Rising Sun, Golden Rays with Rosette by the Emperor of Japan.

By far his most prized possession, however, was his cheetah Chui, which he obtained from a big game hunter in East Africa after visiting the publishing magnate William Randolph Hearst's personal menagerie during a trip to California. Chui was allowed into the house together with Sir Frank's pet fox, but otherwise it lived in a heated outhouse. On one memorable occasion it outran a BBC film crew which tied a rabbit to the back of its van in order to get him going and on occasion Sir Frank would take the big cat out for a drive in the passenger seat of his car. He was eventually persuaded by local police to stop doing this because too many drivers braked to a sudden halt on seeing the two of them out and about.

Rutland

A twelfth-century estate and for more than 400 years home to the Earls of Gainsborough and Viscounts Campden, Exton remains closed to the public although events occasionally take place in the wonderful 1,000-acre park. The family's private nineteenth-century chapel is also used from time to time for Catholic marriage services

The chief joy of the place is neither house nor chapel, however, but rather Fort Henry, a magical fairytale mock-Gothick folly that looks out over a stretch of ornamental water in the park. 'A plastered pleasure house of a most refined and elegant 18th-Century manner,' when commissioned in April 1786 from local Stamford architect William Legg it was known only as the Pond House, and was probably intended by Henry Noel, 6th Earl of Gainsborough, for little more than fishing and picnic parties.

The pinnacled and turreted structure quickly proved a hit, however, and replacing an old boat house it eventually became a lookout from which the Earl and his guests could watch as estate workers re-enacted various famous sea battles, with his lordship observing and ordering the proceedings from the battlements as a number of miniature men-o'-war did battle on the water down below.

Sadly Henry died without issue in 1798, and with him went the earldom. It was revived less than half a century later, however, for an offspring of the female line – unusually for a Catholic grandee the new earl was married four times – and it is still in the same family today. The delightful Fort Henry can be seen from one of the public footpaths which forms part of the Rutland Heritage Trail but may not be visited.

Shropshire

Now the regional headquarters for the National Trust, for much of the post-war period Attingham Park was run by the educational pioneer Sir George Lowthian Trevelyan (1906–96). Regarded by many as one of the founding fathers or even grandfathers of the New Age movement, though wonderfully patrician in appearance he lived a life as far removed as it is possible to be from a traditional, small-c conservative country house-dwelling backwoodsman from the shires.

The fourth in a line of distinguished Northumbrian baronets – with a rumoured connection to one of King Arthur's knights, Sir George was effectively disinherited when his father gave Wallington Hall to the Trust – he was an early student of anthroposophy, an esoteric belief system established by another educational experimentalist, Rudolf Steiner. Intended to aid practitioners in developing their faculties for perceptive imagination, inspiration and intuition through cultivating a form of thinking independent of sensory experience, it was to be one of many '-ologies' and '-osophies' to which Sir George was attracted during his ninety years on the planet.

Already an agnostic when he left Cambridge for a teaching post at his old school (Gordonstoun), Sir George became interested in things spiritual in the early 1940s after drifting into a lecture by a Steiner acolyte. Unusually he combined his intellectual pursuits with a considerable physicality, however, including for more than forty years serving as Master of the strenuous and demanding Lake Hunt. Also known as the Trevelyan Manhunt, this is an annual event devised by a kinsman, the historian G.M. Trevelyan in the 1890s, and still sees a mad dash across such lakeland fells as Great Gable, Kirkfell and Haystacks with scores of human 'hounds' attempting to catch one of four human 'hares'.

When not so engaged Sir George was more interested in conducting his 'exploration of God', viewing the world as 'a living being, in a living universe, a universe which is a great ocean of life and thought' – and diving into that ocean at every possible opportunity to see what he could discover.

His researches were anything but selfish, however, and he rarely lost an opportunity to prick the curiosity of others. At Attingham he took an active interest in every course taught, and leading speakers were invited to speak on subjects as diverse as 'Historic Houses of Britain', 'Finding the Inner Teacher' and 'Death and Becoming'. He was also personally involved in many other organisations, such as the Wrekin Trust which he established in the early 1970s to promote spiritual knowledge and education, and the Findhorn Foundation, an experimental community in Morayshire. A decade later, still hard at it, he was awarded the Right Livelihood Award, a kind of alternative Nobel Prize, for his unstinting work towards 'healing the planet'.

HALSTON HALL, Whittington, nr Oswestry

Not naturally drawn to the academic life, when John Mytton (1796–1834) was prevailed upon to go on to Cambridge after being sacked from both Westminster and Harrow, he did so on the understanding that when he got there he would not be expected to open a single book, let alone read one. Once this was agreed he took steps to arrange for an astonishing 2,000 cases of port to be sent to his new college to await his arrival.

In the end he left them untouched, however, deciding instead to go on a grand tour of the continent before securing a commission in the fashionable 7th Hussars. He spent a lively year in London with the regiment, drinking and gambling, but soon quit after famously celebrating coming into a substantial fortune by jumping his one-eyed charger 'Baronet' over the table in the mess.

By the simple expedient of pinning £10 notes to his coat and encouraging voters to help themselves, he next secured the seat of Shrewsbury but found the workings of Parliament so boring that he remained for just long enough to be sworn in before leaving the Palace of Westminster never to return.

Thereafter he concentrated mostly on drinking and sporting bets and eating filberts – a close relation to the hazelnut – which he consumed in increasingly vast quantities. In the absence of port (of which he was reckoned to have drunk six to eight bottles a day) he'd fasten upon anything else with a similar kick (including it was said eau-de-Cologne if nothing better was on offer). He was also something of a shopaholic, and at one point owned 150 pairs of riding breeches, 700 pairs of riding boots, around a thousand hats and three times that number of made-to-measure shirts.

Despite his daily intake Mytton was up for any sporting challenge which called for physical exertion, although on one occasion he killed his horse by giving it a pint of port to warm it up. Otherwise, in the name of a wager, he was known to wrestle bears, bite dogs, chase rats across frozen lakes, hunt ducks half-naked and once even attempted (unsuccessfully) to jump a tollgate with a coach and four.

Clearly he couldn't go on like this forever, and in the end it all came to a shockingly sudden halt. Just fifteen years after coming into his inheritance Mytton had spent the lot, lost both his seat in Parliament and his ancestral home, and found himself in a debtor's cell. Still only thirty-eight, and in truly terrible shape, one night he set light to his nightshirt in a bizarre attempt to cure an attack of hiccups. It worked, but only because it killed him, and at his funeral an astonishing 3,000 people came by to see him off.

MAWLEY HALL, Cleobury Mortimer

Flat-earthers are reasonably rare, but the devoutly Christian Lady Blount was the real McCoy and stuck by her beliefs until her death in the 1920s. The wife of the elderly Sir Walter de Sodington Blount (1833–1915), she pursued her interests with considerable vigour, even incorporating her ideas into a novel called *Adrian Galilio*. It starred herself – loosely disguised as Lady Alma/Madame Bianka, a 'zetetic lecturer' – together with her husband, the curiously named and cold-hearted Sir Rosemary Alma. Perhaps unsurprisingly it is now long out of print.

In the novel Lady Alma abandons Sir Rosemary for a priest, and in real life Lady Blount also bolted. After providing the old baronet with his heir and a spare, she remarried and hit the lecture circuit to spread the word about her flat-earth beliefs. As head of the Universal Zetetic Society (the word is from the Greek, meaning to seek or proceed through enquiry), she became an ardent pamphleteer as well as publishing, editing and writing most of a monthly magazine, *The Earth*.

Reprising arguments and theories she encountered in the engagingly named but minutely circulated *The Earth Not A Globe Review*, she insisted her own journal was available worldwide – except in Russia where her writings were apparently banned – and claimed a wide readership particularly among clerics and others happy to dismiss the evidence of science.

If nothing else Lady B. was adept at picking the evidence which suited her arguments. For example the new science of photography was recruited to the cause during trips to the Fens and the Old Bedford Level – but many classical demonstrations were dismissed, such as using a pendulum to prove the earth's rotation, or observing the way in which vessels disappear hull-first as they sail over the horizon. She blamed the waves for the fact that the mast was the last bit to disappear, and was rarely known to change her opinions which would be delivered in prose or rhyme depending on her mood with supporting 'evidence' culled from the Bible.

What Sir Walter thought about all this is unknown, but it is hard to avoid the conclusion that he was probably better off keeping out of it. Certainly within the family she was regarded as something of a crank, a view not contradicted by the 12th and last baronet who before his own death in 2004 recalled encounters with the elderly Lady Blount at Mawley when he was just a young boy.

ICKWORTH HOUSE, Horringer, nr Bury St Edmunds (NT)

Now he's safely dead the press sometimes like to describe the 6th Marquess of Bristol as something of a gentleman burglar, a posh but somehow personable rogue like Raffles, perhaps, or Sir Charles Lytton in the original *Pink Panther*. In fact Victor Frederick Cochrane Hervey (1915–85) was a fraudster and serious criminal, Prisoner 19440 spending time in Wormwood Scrubs and HMP Camp Hill after robbing Cartier, and receiving several well-deserved lashes with the cat-o'-nine-tails when this was still legal.

Declared bankrupt while still in his early twenties, after a period selling guns to both sides in the Spanish Civil War, as an inveterate fantasist and liar he went on to hold directorships in a series of shady companies. Following his death in 1985 papers came to light also implicating him in one of the first ever ram-raids. In 1946 his gang had broken into Lord Astor's Hever Castle estate in Kent, escaping with jewels and other artefacts belonging to Henry VIII, Elizabeth I and Anne Boleyn, Bristol afterwards revelled in the title of 'Mayfair's No. 1 Playboy', which he trumpeted in stories about his adventures and exploits that he cheerfully sold to national newspapers of the lowest sort.

His heir, Frederick William John Augustus Hervey (1954–99) – known as John – was perhaps only slightly better, but having had a poor

start in life and such a shocking role model his own fate was perhaps preordained.

His parents divorced when he was only five, his father remarrying twice and presenting him with a three half-siblings, two of whom became models and socialites while the third died tragically young by his own hand following a diagnosis of schizophrenia. For a while things seemed OK, however, and John was a familiar face in society magazines. Seemingly able to defy a miserable upbringing and a father who made little if any attempt to conceal the indifference and even contempt he felt for his first-born, he was for a while a colourful and flamboyant character.

John liked to boast he'd made a fortune – 'the accountants,' he insisted, 'say it is £20,000,000' – but over time it became apparent that the figure if anything indicated how much of his inheritance he had so far squandered. Much of this went on drugs, mostly cocaine and heroin, but with the usual Ferraris and a helicopter thrown in for good measure.

The helicopter he used to buzz his ancestral home at Ickworth, (which had long ago been taken over by the National Trust) the new 7th Marquess had fitted with a loudspeaker so he could hurl foul-mouthed abuse at Trust staff and visitors alike. Personally he cut an increasingly desperate and pathetic figure, and was twice imprisoned for drug offences. In 1998 he sold the remaining lease on one wing of Ickworth back to the Trust – it is now a stylish hotel – and the following year he died, aged forty-four, of AIDS leading to multiple organ failure.

Having once boasted that he was worth £35 million, Bristol's will was in the end probated at £5,000, 'the junkie marquess', as *The Times* called him, having apparently sold all his possessions to feed his addictions and allowed the rest to 'slip through his fingers – every last penny'. He was succeeded by his half brother, also called Frederick William Augustus Hervey.

STOKE COLLEGE, Stoke-by-Clare, nr Sudbury

A classic, storybook miser, Sir Hervey Elwes Bt (1683–1763) of Stoke-by-Clare on the Essex-Suffolk border is to be placed among the richest men in eighteenth-century England. With a fortune equivalent now to around half a billion pounds, he made it his business to get by on no more than 44*s* a week (£2.20) by paying his servants peanuts, wearing his great-great-grandfather's clothes until they fell to pieces, and going to bed with the sun to save on candles.

Fires at Stoke were similarly rarely lit, Sir Hervey keeping warm by pacing up and down furiously; and anyone staying to dinner was offered whatever small game or vermin could be shot on the estate with a single boiled potato on the side. Most guests chose not to repeat the experience of dining with him, the only notable exception being Sir Hervey's nephew, John Meggot, who frequently travelled down from London to do just that.

 The son of a rich Southwark brewer who died when he was only three or four, Meggot had been orphaned when his mother decided to starve herself to death despite inheriting a considerable portfolio of property and bonds. Meggot sensibly determined not to follow suit, and spent some years enjoying the life of fashionable young man about town, friends noting that besides being an enthusiastic gambler he was an informed gourmand and expert on wine.

Visiting Suffolk, however, his demeanour would change completely. Stopping at Chelmsford to change into his shabbiest suit, and dining early to prepare himself for his uncle's meagre fare, he would present himself at Stoke as if his uncle's parsimonious way of living was the most natural thing in the world. By 1763, when he was named as his uncle's sole heir, he seemed to believe it too, eventually changing his name to John Elwes and adopting a largely similar lifestyle.

His inheritance he put to good use, developing a series of magnificent townhouses in some of London's smartest quarters. He refused to enjoy any of the profits, however, keeping just one staff member on the payroll and on occasion eating no more than the reheated corpse of a coot or a stale bun. Over time his home fell into disrepair, his appearance becoming more and more eccentric as he reached deeper into the clothes trunk of his benefactor's great-great-grandfather. On one occasion he adopted a wig he found in a hedge (presumably where it had been abandoned by a tramp) and which he wore beneath a hat stolen from a scarecrow.

Eventually, in old age, his memory began to go the same way as his dress sense, and he made a number of very poor investments. Even so his will dated 1786 mentions property totalling half a million, and when he died some three years later his nephew and two illegitimate sons shared somewhere in the region of £800,000, equivalent perhaps to well over a billion pounds at current values.

Surrey

Built in about 1730 for the 2nd Lord Onslow by the talented Venetian Giacomo Leoni, one of England's most perfect and complete Palladian country houses passed from that family to the National Trust in 1956.

Between times the politically minded Onslows had provided the country with numerous MPs, a Speaker of the House of Commons, a Chancellor of the Exchequer, several Secretaries of State, a Governor for New Zealand, and several Deputy and Chief Whips. More recently the 7th Earl also achieved the distinction of becoming the first hereditary peer to sit on the panel of BBC TV's *Have I Got News For You.*

In fact Michael William Coplestone Dillon Onslow (1938–2011) was on the show twice, proof were it needed that he was both witty and personable, and enabling viewers to see for themselves the kind of colourful throwback which made the House of Lords such an interesting place before the hereditaries were thrown out in favour of the 'day boys' in the reforms of 1999.

Remaining in the Lords a while longer, as one of ninety-two discarded hereditaries who were voted back in as a temporary measure, Onslow cheerfully admitted he was a 'walking advert for reform'. In 2003 he told *Guardian* readers he was 'there as a pustule on the rump of the body politic to remind Mr Blair of unfinished business. I remind the Labour government that it proposed that Lords reform would be in two stages: (1) to get rid of the hereditaries; (2) to give a new second chamber democratic legitimacy.' At the time of writing, of course, the electorate is still waiting for the second part.

In its obituary the *Daily Telegraph* called him 'an unrepentant standard-bearer for the hereditary peerage', the press generally making much of the seventy-three-year-old's preference for loud pink bow-ties, his tendency to quote classical historians, and a wide-ranging taste in music including 'rap, ambient house, acid jazz, jungle and thrash metal'. Tales were similarly retold of his having once galloped a horse along the A3 in Surrey in pursuit of an errant bullock, his purchase of a carved Roman testicle to put beneath his wife's pillow, and his loss of a pet monkey while travelling on the Tube.

Onslow was no fool, however, and although appreciating that in one sense at least he had no place in the Lords he went to great lengths to ensure that as long as he was there his contribution would be meaningful and genuine. This commitment, and of course his own character, meant he was never even remotely apologetic about being one of the hangers-on, memorably telling one Labour life peer 'my peerage is no less democratic because it was recommended by William Pitt than yours, which was proposed by Neil Kinnock.' There is, he said, 'nothing democratic about either.'

With the confidence to express such opinions and so forcefully, it is perhaps unsurprising that Onslow rarely toed a particular party line. The normally Conservative *Daily Mail* was even so quick to observe that with his passing 'Parliament has just lost a good 'un'. For the writer Onslow and others like him represented a welcome diversion from what the paper called the 'lobby-fodder creeps who have been sent to the Lords by recent Prime Ministers' and even now there is still a very real sense that something good and useful was lost with the Labour reforms – and that this loss has yet to be made good.

Onslow himself acknowledged 'the illogicality of [someone] having any power over his fellow citizens just because his forebear got tight with the Prince Regent', but as voters continue to be assailed by unedifying stories of so many time-servers, parliamentary bootlickers, policy wonks, jargon-spouters and expenses-thieves, they can perhaps be forgiven for wondering whether the new Westminster is any better than what went before – or if it ever will be.

DEVIL'S PUNCH BOWL, nr Hindhead (NT)

Sadly it is no longer possible to identify the ramshackle cottage in this celebrated Surrey beauty spot which was once home to a real-life Professor Branestawm. A man of vision who made a fortune in the City, he lost all of it running an experimental school in Cambridge and then settled down to become an inventor of extraordinary imagination and vitality.

Geoffrey Nathaniel Pyke (1893–1943) went into the City after being struck by how stupid-looking most stockbrokers were and concluding that making money in the City must therefore be relatively easy. Before long the money was coming in so thick and fast that he quit broking for good and established his own school in Cambridge. In an environment expressly designed to be nothing like his old school (Wellington, which he hated) his pupils were encouraged to study whatever interested them, and lived free of punishment or reprimand. Unfortunately the place soon ran into money worries, most likely because Pyke was already onto the next stage of his almost comically diverse career.

He joined Combined Operations in time for the Second World War, and devised a new kind of motorised sledge for the Norwegian campaign. (Unfortunately this was too late to be helpful although versions of it did much to advance polar exploration after the war.) His second project was considerable bigger, 'Habbakuk' being its creator's codename for a fleet of vast aircraft carriers, each one more than half a mile long and made of a kind of reinforced ice which he called pykrete.

A mixture of water and wood pulp, Pyke insisted that when frozen solid the material would be stronger than ice, more stable and much less inclined to melt. Pipes circulating cold air through the fuselage would keep the hull permanently frozen, and ships made of it would be virtually unsinkable since bullets would bounce off and even a fast torpedo would likely only make a slight dent in the side.

Hugely enthused by his idea Pyke had a vision of vast flotillas of ships, clad in timber or cork, and suitable for use as transports, floating docks, and even aircraft landing strips. Such craft, he believed, could simply sail into occupied ports, disable enemy vessels by spraying them with supercooled water, and then offload vast blocks of pykrete to block the port once a bridgehead had been secured.

Many brass-hats distrusted the whole idea from the start, but Pyke had a number of supporters in very high places, including Lords Mountbatten and Zuckerman. The latter, as chief scientific adviser to the War Office, admitted Pyke was not a scientist, but saw in him 'a man of a vivid and uncontrollable imagination' whom he liked having on board. Mountbatten went even further, and determined to see Pyke receive a proper hearing once rushed into the PM's private bathroom

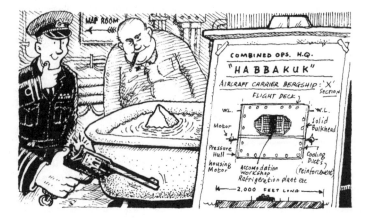

and dropped a lump of pykrete into Winston's tub to demonstrate its resistance to melting. (In a later demonstration he pulled out a revolver and shot it, the resulting ricochet narrowly missing a watching admiral.)

Eventually a prototype ship was built on a Canadian lake, well away from prying eyes. It survived a summer without melting, but with the war drawing towards its conclusion Allied success in the Normandy landings using conventional vessels meant that Habbakuk was sadly never fully put to the test.

Thereafter the few years remaining to Pyke were not happy ones. The ideas kept coming, but interest in them and him waned rapidly and on 21 February 1948 Pyke took to his bed with a bottle of pills and a razor to remove his little goatee beard. It was a strange, sad end to an extraordinary life, but also one characteristic of Pyke who, even as he was slipping in and out of consciousness, kept working away at some notes in his increasingly spidery hand.

PAINSHILL PARK, nr Cobham

The ninth son and fourteenth child born to the 6th Earl of Abercorn, Hon. Charles Hamilton (1704–86) so liked the idea of a hermit that he offered to pay anyone £700 who would live in a cave on his Surrey estate and spend seven years growing a beard. Sadly the only applicant for the job was soon bored to distraction, and after barely a fortnight went off in search of some conversation and a pint of beer.

In the way of these things, Hamilton's enthusiasms had been fired by his grand tour and first manifested themselves in 1738 when he leased some 200 acres of semi-barren heath land close to where the M25 now passes beneath the A3. Ably supported by a share in his father's vast fortune he determined to create a landscape both picturesque to look at and fun to be in, taking as his starting point the paintings of artists such as Claude Lorrain, Salvator Rosa, Poussin and Panini.

To begin with he burned the existing vegetation down to the ground, digging in the resulting piles of ash and having his men grow turnips on the land which in turn he fed to sheep. Their droppings over time raised the level of nutrients in the soil, a slow process but vital as Hamilton, a keen plantsman and an avid collector, was busy importing phenomenal quantities of rare and exotic species to repopulate his land.

At the same time, and at immense expense, the park was landscaped with new valleys being created to open up the right kind of vistas, hills constructed to block off the wrong sort, and a 19-acre ornamental lake excavated around which he arranged an imaginative series of architectural features.

The latter included a grotto, a highly fashionable ten-sided Gothick temple, a Romanesque mausoleum, a ruined abbey, a Turkish tent, another temple (this one dedicated to Bacchus), a Chinese bridge, a bespoke hermitage for the aforementioned, and a wonderful redbrick prospect tower which can still be seen today from the London–Guildford road.

With such a long list one could be forgiven for wondering whether any consideration was given to building a house – and the answer is yes, but only just. Plans for one were not drawn up until 1774, and by the time the architect Richard Jupp got his shoulder to the wheel Painshill had been sold and Hamilton was gone. Creating what Horace Walpole described as 'a fine place out of a most cursed hill' had taken thirty-five years and all his money, and with no further inheritance likely to come his way, the Hon. Charles Hamilton retired instead to Bath.

WITLEY PARK, Witley, nr Godalming

Though now just fragments remain, Witley Park was the creation of a larger-than-life financier called James Whitaker Wright (1846–1904) who created a whimsical fairytale landscape using a fortune made from heavily promoted stock and share issues.

A self-made, self-publicising millionaire, Wright hailed from Cheshire but affected an American accent and eventually wound up at the Royal Courts of Justice where he received a seven-year sentence for twenty-four different counts of fraud. On being sentenced he took a fatal dose of cyanide, a dose he had smuggled into the dock together with a loaded gun.

Before this dismal end Wright had been really flying though, a confident and hugely successful mining and railway entrepreneur who spent his money – or as it turned out other people's – building what is still one of the most beguiling and beautiful man-made landscapes anywhere in the Home Counties.

Sadly the latter is no longer accessible to the public, and the house is mostly gone having catastrophically burned down in the early 1950s. Even so, anyone lucky enough to gain entry to the 500 acres which remain of Wright's 1,400 will find the immense stable courtyard still intact, together with a number of other survivors from Wright's time including decorative eye-catchers and temples scattered around the park. As well as a boat house designed by Lutyens and an incredible 8 acres of walled kitchen garden, Witley boasts Surrey's only underground ballroom beneath one of its four vast ornamental lakes.

As a finishing touch to his million-pound-plus scheme (and this at late nineteenth-century prices) Wright imported from Italy a gigantic bronze sculpture of a dolphin's head. So gigantic indeed that when it was brought up from Southampton docks the contractors had actually to lower the road in order to get it to fit under one of the bridges they passed along the way.

But while this gives some indication as to the scale of Wright's ambitions – and the scope of his landscaping operation – it provides little preparation for Witley's *pièce de résistance*. To get there is quite a journey, made via a secret door in a false tree, through a dark, dank tunnel, down a spiralling ramp and a subterranean flight of steps, along another tunnel – this one flooded, meaning a boat trip 40ft or more below ground level out into the sunlight and across a lake to an artificial island. Once there, yet another staircase takes you down again into the gloom – and there it is.

In truth, once you get there, the aforementioned underwater ballroom is far too small too hold a dance, but it is remarkable even so. Somewhere for guests to have a quiet smoke while watching fish disporting themselves overhead – swimmers too, occasionally – it is Surrey's most eccentric building, far more interesting than the vanished mansion, yet for all that likely to remain forever one of its least known.

Sussex

BATEMANS, nr Burwash (NT)

One of the Trust's smaller properties, this delightful seventeenth-century Wealden house was for nearly forty years home to Rudyard Kipling and his wife and was left to the organisation by the writer's widow on her death in 1939.

The first English-language writer to win the Nobel Prize for Literature (and more than a century on still the youngest), during his lifetime Kipling could reasonably have claimed to have been the world's most widely read author. Such a boast never issued from his lips, however, for always a modest man he famously turned down a knighthood, the Order of Merit and possibly also the post of Poet Laureate. At the height of his career, however, he was reported in the US press to be earning the hitherto unheard of sum of a dollar a word.

Like many writers he had his peculiarities, insisting on ink which was pitch-black, as black as black could be, as the more usual blue-black he considered to be 'an abomination to my daemon'. And while mindful of the need to reach out to his audience – as a journalist he was never less than accessible and enormously popular – he spoke on the wireless only twice, after which he turned down all such invitations.

The latter seems not to have dented his sales much – for a long time *Barrack-Room Ballads* was outselling everything but Shakespeare – but it was a strange decision for someone who was otherwise happy to embrace new innovations. On a trip to the US he adopted the idea of red golf balls so that he could play in the snow, and he was a famously keen early motorist who described the opportunity to explore 'a land full of stupefying marvels and mysteries . . . That is the real joy of motoring – the exploring of this amazing England.'

Kipling in fact became completely hooked on motor cars immediately after taking his first ride in one with a friend, and as early as 1900 imported one of the first steam cars from America which he nicknamed the 'Holy Terror'. Afterwards he developed a passion for British-built Lanchesters, among the first cars to make use of Mr Dunlop's new pneumatic tyres, and which he stuck with despite suffering an incredible twenty-one punctures while driving one home to Sussex from the factory in Birmingham.

For such a private man, particularly after losing his son in the First World War, Kipling also had a surprisingly sharp sense of humour.

After one newspaper erroneously reported his death he wrote to the editor asking to cancel his subscription, and when a canny autograph-hunter sent him a dollar together with a note saying 'I see you get $1 for your writing. Please send me a sample' he replied with an unsigned postcard on which was written just one word: 'Thanks'.

His most moving correspondence was with a French soldier, however, who claimed his life had been saved when his copy of Kipling's *Kim* stopped a bullet. As a token of gratitude the volume was presented to the author, bullet still embedded, together with the soldier's Croix de Guerre. Both were later returned to the soldier after the birth of his son, and the precious paperback is now in the US Library of Congress.

BRIGHTLING PARK, nr Robertsbridge

John 'Mad Jack' Fuller (1757–1834) was a larger-than-life Parliamentarian who was described by the Speaker as 'an insignificant little fellow in a wig' – almost certainly drunk at the time, he actually weighed 22 stone – and later offered a peerage although this was declined. Today, in Brightling at least where the pub still bears his name and arms, he is best remembered for building a gigantic 40ft steeple simply to win a wager.

A keen three-bottles-a-day man, the port-drinking Fuller made the bet after insisting one evening that he could see the spire of St Giles at

Dallington from his windows at Brightling Park. On discovering the following morning that actually he couldn't, he immediately ordered a replica to built and after winning the bet this way seems to have acquired a penchant for largely pointless buildings.

Occasionally these served a secondary purpose, so that while he was impatient of beggars Fuller was nevertheless happy to spend his inheritance taking on the local unemployed and putting them to work. In this way mile after mile of handsome stone walls were constructed around his estate, and at Beachy Head he funded the first Belle Tout Lighthouse while forking out a hefty 3,000 guineas for Bodiam Castle in order to stop the ruins being torn down.

Closer to home he was also responsible for a huge obelisk (known as the Brightling Needle, its summit a full 646ft above sea level), as well as a fine rotunda, and a strange brick pillar. This was topped by an iron flame, a cannon and an anchor as a standing reminder of the iron foundries which accounted for much of the Fuller family fortune.

With such a track record it was perhaps inevitable that the unmarried Mad Jack would save the best until last, and after a good life he chose to be buried in a huge pyramid designed for him by Sir Robert Smirke, architect of the British Museum.

Sir Robert had earlier built an observatory for his client, but the pyramid looks the finer piece, its chief purpose according to Fuller being to prevent him being eaten by his own family. Without it, he explained, 'the worms will eat me, the ducks will eat the worms and my relatives will eat the ducks.' Instead, much in the manner of Charlemagne, Mad Jack is in his mausoleum still, seated upright on an iron chair, carefully positioned before a table holding a roast chicken and a bottle of port – and surrounded by broken glass 'so that when the devil comes for me he might at least cut his feet.'

PETWORTH HOUSE, Petworth (NT)

According to those who knew him, the nickname bestowed on Charles Seymour, 6th Duke of Somerset (1662–1748) – the Proud Duke – was well deserved, and from the earliest age. Handsome, inordinately fond of ceremonials in which he had a role to play and extremely vain, Seymour was already well on his way to becoming an insufferable, preening peacock and on marrying Elizabeth Percy he looked in danger of tipping over the edge.

The heiress to the ancient wealth and titles of the Earls of Northumberland, including six of the oldest baronies in England, if nothing else Elizabeth's dowry enabled His Grace to indulge his passion for pomp and ceremony. Also, alas, the chance to give in to a new and worrying belief that the lower orders were unfit even to look at him, an affectation which saw the historian Thomas Macaulay describe him as, 'a man in whom the pride of birth and rank amounted almost to a disease.'

This would have been bad enough on its own, but unfortunately Somerset's definition of what constituted the 'lower orders' embraced just about everyone he ever met. Even his own children were unable to escape the classification, and one of his daughters, having once had the temerity to sit down in his presence, promptly found herself deprived of an inheritance equivalent to £20 or £30 million today.

Given that, it is little wonder that the great unwashed were so far beyond the pale, and that he refused completely to talk to them or have any dealings with the public aside from issuing the occasional order via a form of sign language or gesture.

Unlike the reclusive 5th Duke of Portland (see p. 120) Seymour's icy silence had nothing whatever to do with his being shy and retiring, however. He was a snob, pure and simple, and one who went to extraordinary lengths to avoid the masses, so offended was he by the mere idea that somebody ordinary might even glimpse his magnificence.

To a lesser or perhaps less pompous individual this might have involved spending his time at Petworth – previously a Percy stronghold – and never venturing beyond its tall walls. Alternatively he could have tunnelled his way out, like Portland planned to do, or simply drawn the blinds on his carriage so no-one could peer in as he made his way to town.

But nothing so simple appealed to such a mad, overbearing tyrant as His Grace, and instead the construction of a whole series of houses was authorised along the routes from Sussex and his other estates into London. Ensuring he had somewhere clean and private to break his journey, they proved a handy place for him to tarry while outriders went on ahead to clear the route of commoners before the Proud Duke set out on the next leg of his journey.

COTON HOUSE, Churchover, nr Rugby

The last private owner of this small but fine late-eighteenth-century house by Samuel Wyatt, Venetia James (1855–1948) was rich and exceptionally well-connected but was painstaking when it came to scrimping and was rarely if ever embarrassed by her reputation as the most county's most notoriously cheeseparing niggard.

Born a Cavendish-Bentinck – a direct descendant of the 3rd Duke of Portland – her marriage to the son of a Manchester millionaire made her richer still. This enabled the newlyweds to take a long lease on this 500-acre estate near Rugby where they entertained on a lavish scale and built a hugely successful stud. In 1907 a visit by Queen Victoria's youngest child, Princess Henry of Battenberg, provided an excuse to build a new guest suite and conservatory; two years later Edward VII chose to stay at Coton, during a tour of the area.

Things changed decisively following the death of husband Arthur James in 1917, however, and once widowed Venetia lost no opportunity to save money or to let guests know how much their visits were costing her. Local tradesmen were prevailed upon to offer everything on a sale-or-return basis – years later a great-nephew recalled his great-aunt sending Saturday night's leftovers back to the butcher – and she was said to prefer entertaining Catholics to others on a Friday night because fish was cheaper than meat. On other occasions the butler would be passed a note reading DCSC, meaning 'don't cut the second chicken', Venetia having decided that her guests had already eaten quite enough.

There was certainly money in the coffers – in 1936, after leasing the estate for nearly half a century, the widow bought it outright – but her determination not to waste it was such that, having been invited to tea, another young relative heard her telling the maid Emily, 'if the cat has left any of its milk, bring it up now.' (Subsequently the same servant was ordered to 'discommand the cat's meat' when her mistress returned home from a walk in the park with a dead sparrow which she felt would serve just as well.)

Her stinginess with food was perhaps the most remarked upon of her own eccentricities, because as an economy it impacted on those around her. But to her credit Mrs James was just as happy to economise when it came to herself, and she was frequently to be observed standing on

the platform at Rugby station waiting for a train with the cheapest third-class accommodation rather than climbing on the first one in and walking to the front.

In fact only one of Venetia's regular bills was paid in full and on time, and that was the one presented by the veterinarian who looked after the racehorses she continued to breed until well into old age. That said, even with this chap she attempted to strike a bargain, once asking him to examine one of the maids while he was at it as she had always felt doctors to be a scandalous waste of money.

West Midlands

Another inveterate inventor, Thomas Thorneycroft (1822–1903) was also another fresh air freak who installed an estimated sixty different air pumps and ventilators around the family home at Tettenhall. Pleased with the result he set forth for the capital where he hoped to pipe clean air in from the coast and charge Londoners by the cubic foot via his new Fresh Air Joint Stock Company.

When shares in the company proved unpopular – in fact he found no takers at all – he returned home, and between fathering '30 feet of boys and quite 21 of girls' (nine children in all) Thorneycroft set about devising an array of curious gadgets in the hope that some would prove profitable.

His sprung floor for the ballroom was reasonably effective, so too the heated shoe-case for drying out damp footwear. His version of a dumb-waiter worked well too although few if any householders felt inclined to follow his example and relocate the kitchen above the dining room in order to reduce the transmission of cooking smells. A newly patented design for a chimney also failed to catch on, potential customers presumably failing to share his enthusiasm for the 10ft-high flames which resulted from his system of mechanically induced draughts.

Thorneycroft's attempts at flight were also dogged by disaster, although he was at least shrewd enough to get his butler to leap off

the roof at Tettenhall wearing a pair of home-made wings rather than attempting the flight himself. And while on one occasion out ballooning he managed to avoid being sucked into a factory chimney, he found no customers for the kind of balloon-mounted fan he had devised to avoid any such thing happening again.

The Admiralty was similarly not noticeably interested in his plan to equip its ships with vast steam-guns able to fire scalding gas jets at incoming vessels – conventional naval guns seemed altogether easier – and the people of Shrewsbury were similarly quick to dismiss his scheme to create a 'Henley of the Midlands' on the Severn. But through it all Thorneycroft seems to have remained undaunted, displaying that combination of self-confidence and self-containment which so often mark out the truly, irredeemably odd.

Wiltshire

The most extreme and perhaps best known British tower-builder, William Beckford (1759–1844) famously plied his workforce with free beer in a bid to get them to work round the clock on his near-300ft high Fonthill Abbey. Predictably but calamitously the finished structure was so poorly built that it collapsed not once but twice, but even had it survived its status as Britain's largest folly (and Europe's tallest private house) would doubtless have secured Beckford's reputation as an eccentric of the highest quality.

Just ten years old when his father died, Beckford inherited the Wiltshire estate in 1770 together with a fortune said to have been worth a million and yielding an annual dividend of around £100,000. Sufficient to make him a dangerously rich little boy, the source of it was extensive sugar plantations in Jamaica, a source which went on to pay for a life of excess which few since have been able to match.

Though a commoner Beckford travelled in state and in style with a retinue typically comprising three footmen, twenty-four musicians, his doctor, a valet, a cook, two dogs – Mrs Fry and Viscount Fartleberry – and a personal dwarf imported from Spain. Over a period of fifteen years, his itinerary was impressive, and it introduced him to a wealth of different architectural influences – such as the monastery and abbey church at Batalha, Portugal, – which bubbled to the top when he settled down to design Fonthill.

More than anything he wanted Fonthill to be enormous, and centred on an octagonal tower 300ft high. Skimping on foundations meant it took only six years to complete – and of course just seconds to collapse – whereupon the eccentric Beckford shrugged off the disaster, contacted his bankers and called everyone back to have another go.

This time, he insisted, it was all going to be different, with better materials, a longer build-time to ensure everything was done correctly, and some proper foundations. Fonthill Mark II at least lasted long enough for him to move in – and for JMW Turner to paint it so we know what it looked like. But sadly it too collapsed eventually, albeit only after it had been sold to the unfortunate John Farquhar, an untidy millionaire who dressed atrociously and it was said delighted in being mistaken for a tramp.

Before he moved out Beckford had a marvellous time, entertaining Lord Nelson on one occasion and on another a trespasser, who had somehow succeeded in scaling the 7-mile-long, 12ft-high walls which Beckford had built around his estate. But as often as not the dinners held beneath the octagon took a far stranger turn, the table being laid for twelve, food and drink being laid on for twelve, and twelve footmen standing firm behind twelve chairs – before their employer sat down to dine alone.

When the time came to sell – he was virtually bankrupt, but managed to relieve Farquhar of £330,000 – Beckford moved to Bath, building another tower, this time just 120ft tall in his garden at Lansdowne Crescent. Designed by a trained architect it's happily still standing: a steep 200 steps taking visitors to the summit where the whole is crowned by an elegant replica of the Athenian Monument of Lysicrates.

H.E. Goodridge's 1827 design originally incorporated a library and a chapel as well niches in the walls in which (it is said) Beckford's maids were expected to cower as the rampantly misogynistic Beckford passed by. In time the garden – exceedingly narrow but almost a mile long – became a private graveyard, with a marble tomb erected for another Beckford dog (Tiny) and once the legal niceties had been completed to enable him to lie in unconsecrated ground a pink granite sarcophagus for her extraordinary master.

Worcestershire

From an auctioneer's point of view the best person to have in the room when selling off a bibliomaniac's library is another bibliomaniac, and while in Richard Heber's case it must have seemed highly unlikely a buyer could be found to match the zeal of the seller, history shows that Sir Thomas Phillips of Middle Hall, Broadway came a good deal closer than most.

Heber (1776–1833) had started early, and by the age of eight already had a library and had catalogued everything in it. After studying at Oxford he began adding to this in earnest, driven not just by his desire to own every book, manuscript and document he could get his hands on but by a firm conviction that, 'no gentleman can be without three copies of a book, one for show, one for use, and a third at the service of his friends.'

To keep pace he bought in bulk, once acquiring 30,000 volumes in a single sale and maintaining eight different houses – in London, the English countryside and on the continent – in which to store his treasures. Walter Scott praised his library to the skies, but despite Heber's willingness to share he was widely derided, and at times compared to an addict on the grounds that 'no confirmed drunkard, no incurable opium-eater has less control.'

On the other hand it was his own money, and with no-one to share it – curiously he never married – he was free to spend, and did so with abandon. Acquiring more than 150,000 publications cost him well over £100,000 at eighteenth-century prices, with one visitor at one of Heber's houses describing an unholy jumble and how 'up to the very ceiling the piles of volumes extended, while the floor was strewn with them in loose and numerous heaps.'

At his death the bulk of the collection realised barely half as much at auction, but in today's terms it still represented tens of millions of pounds, the majority of which was contributed by the aforementioned Phillips.

Heber's junior by a good thirty years, and memorably described in a memoir called *Portrait of an Obsession*, Sir Thomas Phillips reputedly never discarded anything on paper, and by middle-age had collected more ancient manuscripts than were held in the British Library or at Oxford or Cambridge universities. Like Heber he too bought in bulk; unlike Heber he managed to secure a wife and to father three daughters. All four were recruited to help catalogue his overflowing collection, the family living like misers in order to feed his addiction, and the only money not spent on books being set aside to employ a personal printer to produce his catalogues. With most estate buildings by this time fallen down through lack of care, the printer himself was housed in the late eighteenth-century Broadway Tower, then a ruinous, windswept folly on the Phillips estate rather than the splendid belvedere it is today.

As a buyer Phillips always drove a hard bargain, but then frequently refused to cough up. He was eventually forced abroad to escape his creditors, who by this time included most of the antiquarian booksellers in England. Incredibly the printer kept hard at it though, even learning Latin and Old English in order to keep on top of his employer's voluminous and recondite purchases.

Eventually Sir Thomas's father-in-law stepped in to save the day, clearing the debts on the estate but sadly not before his daughter had collapsed under the strain. She died, aged thirty-seven, and on returning to England Sir Thomas admitted to a friend he needed money more than a companion and that any wife could have him who was worth £50,000. Amazingly, ten years later, after as many as seventeen refusals, he found one worth £3,000 a year which he took in the hope he could realise the rest by 'selling' his daughters.

Unfortunately, and on little or no evidence, his first son-in-law he took to be a book-thief, Phillips taking drastic action to protect his treasures. Everything on the estate which could be was sold, after which a team of

230 dray horses spent days pulling 100 wagons piled high with books across the Cotswolds to another, more rackety house. With his collection soon overrun with rats, his second wife understandably went mad and left. For his part, Sir Thomas just went mad, declaring to anyone who would listen 'I wish to have one copy of every book in the world!!!!!' and pursuing this foolish and impossible goal until his death at the age of eighty.

Yorkshire

For the 5th Duke of Portland (*q.v.*) a 2ft black hat and several coats provided a means of disguise, but for Sir Tatton Sykes (1826–1913) the extra layers were more about maintaining a stable local as he believed that there was no safer route to good health than ensuring a constant body temperature.

Convinced that overheating constituted a dangerous assault on his personal wellbeing, Sir Tatton typically left home wearing several overcoats, shedding them one by one as the day progressed in a bid to remain at the temperature he was when he first walked out. His coats were therefore ordered in number of colours and different sizes – each being large enough to fit comfortably over the preceding one – with a similar arrangement for his trousers. If things got too hot he was likely to discard his socks and shoes and stick his feet out of the window and was frequently observed doing precisely this.

Naturally he had no intention of carrying the garments he discarded in this way. He was a Yorkshire grandee, after all, and the extra exertion

might have caused his temperature to climb. Instead he had a standing arrangement with local juveniles that anyone returning a coat or a pair of trousers to the kitchens at Sledmere would be rewarded with a shilling and a hot meal. In this way he was free to drop his clothes where and whenever he chose, shedding layers as he went about his business while being reasonably sure the items would eventually find their way home.

While by no means a bad landlord Sir Tatton also had a thing about flowers, which he thought 'nasty, untidy things'. Any he found growing on his walks he cheerfully beheaded with a swish of his cane, and while ploughing up his own beds and lawns after inheriting Sledmere he warned tenants on his estate that if they must grow flowers these should be restricted to cauliflowers. Most seemed prepared to go along with this, and also Sir Tatton's more bizarre request that from now on they should lock their front doors and use only the back ones.

WALTON HALL, nr Harrogate

With an interest in wildlife and the money to indulge it, Charles Waterton (1782–1865) returned from his travels in South America where, having encountered such exotica as chameleons, lemurs, sunbirds and alligators, he conceived a plan to create what was almost certainly the world's first ever wildlife sanctuary.

Needless to say he didn't call it that at the time, but having 'suffered and learnt mercy' while recovering from yellow fever he found himself firmly opposed to the destruction of any wildlife and ordered his estate accordingly. It was an eccentric notion in an age when hunting, shooting and fishing were meat and drink to most country squires, but undeterred Waterton set about building a private nature reserve at Walton Hall.

His first move was to construct 3 miles of stone wall around the estate, as much to keep the wildlife in as the poachers out. By his own account it cost him £9,000, a phenomenal sum at the time and one which Waterton claimed to have saved by giving up wine, and by eating little more than dry toast and watercress. (Such an ascetic lifestyle began to grow on him, and following the death of his wife he spent thirty-five years sleeping on the floor with a wooden block for a pillow.)

Keen to encourage wildlife to thrive he installed artificial nesting boxes at intervals – a world first, and his own innovation – as well as importing rare owls from Italy in the hope that these would breed. He also instructed his foresters to leave any hollow logs or branches where they lay to provide other nesting places for birds and invertebrates – an inspired idea at the time although one which these days landowners take for granted.

It was inside the hall, however, that things got really weird. Waterton's collection of household pets at various times included an albino hedgehog, a duck without the usual webbed feet, a species of toad he had collected in Brazil, and a three-toed sloth. Sometimes Waterton would also pretend to be some species or other himself, dropping down onto all fours and nipping at visitors' ankles as they waited in the hall.

Naturally curious, for a while he kept a vampire bat in his bedroom and in the hope that it would bite him – he was especially keen to write up the symptoms – and routinely slept with one foot, temptingly unstockinged, poking out from under the covers. Sadly the bat refused to play ball, however, and instead bit an Indian servant so that the experiment was judged a failure.

Oddly his respect for his animals didn't go beyond the grave, however, and once dead all such pets were quickly stuffed, mounted and put on display. One gorilla was even dissected at dinner, on the dining room table between the cheese and port, and if Waterton ever felt the finished result was insufficiently interesting he would cheerfully mix and match different parts from different animals until he had achieved the desired effect.

Examples included the Noctifer, which combined bits of an eagle owl with parts from a bittern; the Nondescript (an air-dried howler monkey looking disturbingly like an eskimo mummy); and a peculiar horned monkey which was said to represent Martin Luther after his fall. Perhaps the weirdest was something Waterton described as 'John Bull and the National Debt' in which a vaguely human face was applied to the body of a porcupine and half-concealed beneath the shell of a tortoise and some pocket-sized devils.

Such eccentricities aside, many of Waterton's ideas were clearly years ahead of their time, and contemporary reports suggest he had a genuinely special bond with species other than his own. Unfortunately Waterton's sentiments were not shared by his family. Following his death at the age of eighty-three his son Edmund held a number of shooting parties on the estate, with predictable results for the wildlife. Eventually the estate was broken up and sold and more recently Walton Hall reopened as an hotel. Waterton himself is buried somewhere in the grounds, apparently between two favourite trees, while his Noctifer, the Nondescript and a number of his other strange creature-creations were rescued and put on display at Wakefield Museum.

Other titles published by The History Press

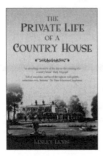

The Private Life of a Country House
LESLEY LEWIS

ISBN 978-0-7524-6051-2

In this vivid memoir Lesley Lewis gives a lucid account of how family life was lived in an English country house between the wars. The elaborate daily rhythm of the household, and the devoted skill of the servants who ran it, are faithfully brought back to life. Well illustrated by drawings and photographs, the result is an intriguing glimpse into the recent English past.

Random Acts of Politeness
Eccentric, Quirky and Occasionally Suicidal Examples of Selflessness and Courtesy

ANDREW TAYLOR

ISBN 978-0-7524-5977-6

Chivalrous, noble and selfless acts which transcend class, wealth and age – this uplifting collection of true anecdotes will make yo wonder what people really mean when they say manners maket man.

When Did Big Ben First Bong?
101 questions answered about the greatest city on earth

DAVID LONG

ISBN 978-0-7524-5584-6

Do you know when Big Ben first bonged – or even who Ben was. Why the River Thames is so-called? Who had the worst ever 'mockney' accent? From the truth about Handel's ugly ears to hippos running wild in Trafalgar Square, it's all in *When Did Big Ben First Bong?*, the ultimate trivia guide to the greatest city on Earth.

Visit our website and discover thousands of other History Press books.

www.thehistorypress.co.uk